"An accessible introduction to the questio ably hitting a center position that sees asp important, and yet not oversimplifying tl place to start investigating this important i.

—William D. Mounce, author of *Basics of Biblical Greek*

"This is the accessible treatment of verbal aspect we have been waiting for! In a field which can be overly technical, Dr. Campbell has provided a lucid, readable and short introduction that will be enormously helpful for students and their professors. His explanations of concepts are clear, his model of how to move from aspect to kind of action portrayed is wonderfully useful, and his examples are well chosen. Bravo!"

—Steve Walton, Senior Lecturer in Greek and New Testament Studies, London School of Theology

"Students of New Testament Greek have for years been wrestling with middle-level and advanced volumes unpacking verbal aspect. Something of a revolution has taken place during the last two decades. What has been lacking, however, has been an accessible introduction to the subject. Here it is! With limpid prose, logical development, and helpful examples, Con Campbell has put countless teachers and students in his debt."

—D. A. Carson, Research Professor of New Testament, Trinity Evangelical Divinity School

"Campbell and I agree on at least one major point regarding verbal aspect: understanding Greek verbal aspect is crucial for understanding the Greek of the New Testament. For too long such knowledge has been woefully lacking among commentators and other students of the New Testament. One cannot exegete the text responsibly without applying an accurate understanding of Greek verbal aspect. If this book helps students and scholars to realize this crucial point, it will have accomplished its purpose."

—Stanley E. Porter, President and Dean, and Professor of New Testament, McMaster Divinity College; author, *Verbal Aspect of the Greek of the New Testament, with Reference to Tense and Mood*

"Dr. Campbell's masterly introduction to verbal aspect in biblical Greek will be appreciated by teachers and students of the New Testament alike. His clear examples of this complex but important subject, the pertinent examples he provides, and how verbal aspect contributes to our exegesis and translation, all make this volume a must for those who want to study the New Testament in Greek."

—Peter T. O'Brien, Senior Research Fellow in New Testament, Moore College

"This is a book that I wish I had had the foresight (and time!) to write.... This volume extends the discussion further by including a systematic method for working with both aspect and *Aktionsart*. To my knowledge, this is the first time this has been done, and the result, though not exhaustive, appears to provide a sane and solid foundation for using both these theoretical constructs in a complementary way for New Testament exegesis."

—Rodney J. Decker, Professor of Greek and New Testament, Baptist Bible College and Seminary; author, *Temporal Deixis of the Greek Verb in the Gospel of Mark with Reference to Verbal Aspect*

Basics

of

VERBAL ASPECT

in

Biblical Greek

CONSTANTINE R. CAMPBELL

ZONDERVAN

Basics of Verbal Aspect in Biblical Greek
Copyright © 2008 by Constantine R. Campbell

This title is also available as a Zondervan ebook.
Visit www.zondervan.com/ebooks.

Requests for information should be addressed to:

Zondervan, 3900 *Sparks Dr. SE, Grand Rapids, Michigan 49546*

Library of Congress Cataloging-in-Publication Data

Campbell, Constantine R.
        Basics of verbal aspect in biblical Greek / Constantine R. Campbell.
            p. cm.
        Includes index.
        ISBN 978-0-310-29083-4 (softcover)
            1. Greek language, Biblical—Verb. 2. Greek language, Biblical—Aspect. I. Title.
PA847.C35 2008
487'.4—dc22   2008026373

Any Internet addresses (websites, blogs, etc.) and telephone numbers in this book are offered as a resource. They are not intended in any way to be or imply an endorsement by Zondervan, nor does Zondervan vouch for the content of these sites and numbers for the life of this book.

Cover design: *Tammy Johnson*
Interior design: *Mark Sheeres*

Printed in the United States of America

HB 01.29.2024

For my parents

John and Malamatenie Campbell

Contents

Preface

The study of verbal aspect has been around for a long time. Since the middle of the nineteenth century, verbal aspect has been an interest of language scholars, including those who were working with Ancient Greek. So, it's no recent fad. But if that's the case, it seems odd that verbal aspect is not more widely understood and appreciated by students of Greek. There does seem to be a kind of general awareness within the community of informed Greek teachers and students of something "out there" called verbal aspect. But it's tricky, unknown, and a bit scary.

The most likely reason that verbal aspect has not really taken root in the way Greek is taught and studied is that the majority of the literature about it is highly technical and somewhat controversial. Even when a student makes the effort to plough through some of the heavy material on the subject, the practical implications for translation and exegesis may still seem less than apparent.

While there are still issues to be ironed out and debated at the academic level—as is the case for many areas of research—there is enough common ground for it to be taught at the student level. Even a basic handle on verbal aspect is worthwhile for those interested in exegesis and translation of Greek text. In order to achieve this, I've thought for some time that what we really need is a primer on Greek verbal aspect—an introduction, a textbook, a way in for nonspecialists. That's what we've tried to provide with this book.

I'm grateful to Zondervan for sharing the vision for a book like this, and in particular I'm indebted to Verlyn Verbrugge. Verlyn has shown great enthusiasm from beginning to end, and his meticulous editorial work is immensely appreciated. It's fair to say that this book would not exist without him. Thanks must also go to Moisés Silva for his insightful critique of an early draft.

A myriad of others have contributed in various ways. Colleagues and students at Moore College have helped to shape and improve the material that now forms this book. In particular, I'm grateful to Richard Gibson, who taught aspect with me, for his pedagogical suggestions and insights that have been invaluable for pitching it at the right level. Thanks also to

Bill Salier and Philip Kern, who have been teaching this material alongside me too. Other colleagues who have supported and encouraged me through this project include Peter Bolt, Brian Rosner, and Peter O'Brien—many thanks.

To the students of Moore College (past and present), I am thankful for the many questions and suggestions that have sharpened my teaching of verbal aspect in various ways. I also appreciate the energy and enthusiasm with which they have tackled the subject. Special thanks goes to Anthony Kerr, Naomi Ireland, Ben Hudson, Chris Spark, Rick Hall, Vivian Cheung, Peter Orr, Jonathan Howes, Chris Swann, Scott Lovell, John Bartik, Jonny Gibson, Anne-Sophie Rowcroft, Mike Southon, Ben May, Stephen Bell, Kristan Slack, and Bernie Cane.

I am ever grateful for my wife, Bronwyn, and our children, Jasmine, Xanthe, and Lukas, who endure projects such as this with patience and love.

This book is dedicated to my parents, John and Malamatenie Campbell. One has a special interest in Greek, the other in the New Testament. Both are lifelong teachers.

Soli Deo Gloria

Verbal Aspect and Exegesis

—◦◦◦—

Why Verbal Aspect?

Some people who pick up this book will need no encouragement to read it in its entirety. They know that verbal aspect in biblical Greek is a matter to be dealt with. They understand that verbal aspect represents a controversial area of research, which has potentially wide-ranging exegetical implications. They also know that most publications about verbal aspect are written by specialists *for* specialists, and that there is a lot of confusion surrounding the topic for everyone else. Yet they want to understand. They want to know what all the fuss is about and why it matters. Will verbal aspect affect exegesis and translation? Will it change the way we read the Bible? How will it change things, and to what extent?

Such people will welcome a book like this and may even have skipped the introduction and moved straight into the business part of the book.

But what about the reader who is not convinced that reading a book like this is worth the time and investment? Perhaps the student for whom this book has been allocated as required reading in a Greek course, but is otherwise not all that interested. Perhaps the pastor who wants to keep up to speed with their Greek, but wonders if tackling verbal aspect is worth it. Perhaps the New Testament scholar who is not yet convinced that verbal aspect represents an improvement on the way they learned Greek years ago and have taught it for years.

Here are some of the questions I have encountered about verbal aspect. What difference does it really make to get verbal aspect right? Is this whole enterprise just something to challenge the academic mind with fine nuances that do not bear directly on exegesis and exposition? Are the results much different from those reached by earlier approaches to the verbal system? And if not, what's the point of it all? Let's be frank: some readers have probably approached this subject with the most important question of all in mind: "So what?"

This introduction explores some of the exegetical implications and applications that may be derived from verbal aspect. It may seem a little strange to attempt to do this at the beginning of the book. We haven't even addressed what verbal aspect *is* yet. But because I think it's important to try to show why verbal aspect matters, we will raise some questions about Greek verbs without trying to answer them at this stage. Raising the questions themselves will, I think, satisfy the "so what?" question. To achieve this, our undertaking will be characterized by two approaches. We will approach the implications of aspect for exegesis from both a negative and positive standpoint.

From a negative point of view, a good understanding of verbal aspect will enable us to assess and critique some of the scholarly conclusions reached about various Greek passages. New Testament commentaries frequently engage with the Greek text as a matter of course and often build the case for their conclusions using arguments arising from their understanding of Greek verbs. These conclusions then filter down to sermons heard in church on Sunday. Pastors consult the commentaries and shape their message around the conclusions reached there. Sermons affect the understanding of church folk, who take their pastors' conclusions to their home group Bible studies, and before we know it the view that originated in the commentary has become folklore. But what if the original argument was flawed? What if the argument hinged on a misinformed understanding of the Greek verbal system? What if our understanding of God's Word has been distorted, even just a little, by incorrect handling of Greek verbs?

Do you think such a phenomenon is rare? It's more common than you may think. Understanding Greek verbs matters. It does make a difference, as we will see.

From a positive point of view, a good understanding of verbal aspect will enable us to see how narratives are shaped by verbs and to see new possibilities for exegesis that were previously hidden from view. We will be able to describe verbal usage in a manner that is accurate, coherent, and neither too much nor too little. All these things represent a useful advance.

Negative Insights

In commentaries and sermons certain tendencies are clearly evident when it comes to the use of some Greek verbs. In this section, I suggest that such tendencies are unhelpful and at times misleading. Consider the following examples.

Romans 5:6 Ἔτι γὰρ Χριστὸς ὄντων ἡμῶν ἀσθενῶν ἔτι κατὰ καιρὸν ὑπὲρ ἀσεβῶν **ἀπέθανεν**.

*For while we were still weak, at the right time Christ **died** for the ungodly.*

Some commentators write that because an aorist is used here, Romans 5:6 proves that Christ's death was a once-for-all event, never to be repeated, and therefore Christ could not be reoffered time and time again (as in the Roman mass). While I do not want to deny the once-for-all nature of Christ's death (cf. 1 Peter 3:18), the aorist in Romans 5:6 does not prove the point at all. Why not? Because that's not what an aorist means. People who argue such things about this verse base their argument on a faulty understanding of the aorist indicative. A proper understanding of verbal aspect avoids such an error.[1]

1 Timothy 2:12 διδάσκειν δὲ γυναικὶ **οὐκ ἐπιτρέπω** οὐδὲ αὐθεντεῖν ἀνδρός, ἀλλ᾽ εἶναι ἐν ἡσυχίᾳ.

*I do **not** **permit** a woman to teach or to have authority over a man; instead, she is to be silent.*

Some recent attempts to explain this controversial verse have resorted to the meaning of the present indicative as key to their interpretation. The argument states that the present indicates an action in progress. As such, Paul does not permit this action *at the time of his writing*—he currently does not permit women to teach or to have authority over a man. But this is the current situation for Paul; it does not speak to our current situation, because that would not make sense of the present indicative.

Whatever one makes of this verse and the arguments surrounding it, it is clear that this particular argument is misleading insofar as it is based on an erroneous understanding of the verb.

---

1. Carson helpfully lists a catalogue of exegetical errors made by scholars with reference to the aorist indicative. See D. A. Carson, *Exegetical Fallacies* (2nd ed.; Grand Rapids: Baker, 1996), 68–73.

John 17:17 ἀγίασον αὐτοὺς ἐν τῇ ἀληθείᾳ· ὁ λόγος ὁ σὸς ἀλήθειά ἐστιν.

Sanctify them by the truth; your word is truth.

The aorist imperative in this verse has been taken by some to prove that sanctification is an instantaneous event. This is especially the case within the so-called holiness movement, which asserts that Christians are made morally pure at the moment of conversion. It is argued that because aorist imperatives issue commands that are to be performed instantaneously, this verse and others like it provide evidence to support the concept of instantaneous sanctification. This is yet another error that has arisen from misunderstanding verbs.[2]

There are many similar examples of exegesis to be found throughout commentaries, sermons, and the like. Some of these exegetical mistakes arise from common misapplications of traditional theories that have to do with the Greek verbal system. Others arise from correct applications of theories that have been shown to be lacking, imprecise, or just plain wrong. To do responsible exegesis and translation, we simply must understand Greek verbs better.

Positive Insights

The ability to critique earlier patterns of exegesis is not the only benefit to be derived from the study of Greek verbal aspect. There are, of course, many positive advances in understanding the New Testament that may be ventured.

One type of positive advance is being able to articulate why certain verbs are used within their particular contexts. Consider the following passage.

John 7:28–32 ἔκραξεν οὖν ἐν τῷ ἱερῷ διδάσκων ὁ Ἰησοῦς καὶ λέγων· κἀμὲ οἴδατε καὶ οἴδατε πόθεν εἰμί· καὶ ἀπ᾽ ἐμαυτοῦ οὐκ ἐλήλυθα, ἀλλ᾽ ἔστιν ἀληθινὸς ὁ πέμψας με, ὃν ὑμεῖς οὐκ οἴδατε· ἐγὼ οἶδα αὐτόν, ὅτι παρ᾽ αὐτοῦ εἰμι κἀκεῖνός με ἀπέστειλεν. Ἐζήτουν οὖν αὐτὸν πιάσαι, καὶ οὐδεὶς ἐπέβαλεν ἐπ᾽ αὐτὸν τὴν χεῖρα, ὅτι οὔπω ἐληλύθει ἡ ὥρα αὐτοῦ. Ἐκ τοῦ ὄχλου δὲ πολλοὶ ἐπίστευσαν εἰς αὐτὸν καὶ ἔλεγον· ὁ χριστὸς ὅταν ἔλθῃ μὴ πλείονα σημεῖα ποιήσει ὧν οὗτος ἐποίησεν; ἤκουσαν οἱ Φαρισαῖοι τοῦ

---

2. See Randy L. Maddox, "The Use of the Aorist Tense in Holiness Exegesis," *Weslyan Theological Journal* 16 (1981), 168–79.

ὄχλου γογγύζοντος περὶ αὐτοῦ ταῦτα, καὶ ἀπέστειλαν οἱ ἀρχιερεῖς καὶ οἱ Φαρισαῖοι ὑπηρέτας ἵνα πιάσωσιν αὐτόν.

As he was teaching in the temple complex, Jesus cried out, "You know me and you know where I am from. Yet I have not come on my own, but the One who sent me is true. You don't know him; I know him because I am from him, and he sent me." Then they tried to seize him. Yet no one laid a hand on him because his hour had not yet come. However, many from the crowd believed in him and said, "When the Messiah comes, he won't perform more signs than this man has done, will he?" The Pharisees heard the crowd muttering these things about him, so the chief priests and the Pharisees sent temple police to arrest him.

Why are the aorist indicatives ἔκραξεν, ἐπέβαλεν, ἐπίστευσαν, ἤκουσαν, and ἀπέστειλαν used for actions that outline the basic events of this narrative? And then, why are the imperfects ἐζήτουν and ἔλεγον, and the pluperfect ἐληλύθει, used for descriptive and explanatory parts of the narrative? Why are the perfects οἴδατε [x2], ἐλήλυθα, and οἶδα only found within direct speech? Prior to advances in our understanding of verbal aspect, it would have been difficult to give good explanations for these fairly typical phenomena.

Another type of positive advance comes through the opening of new exegetical possibilities.

2 Timothy 4:6–7 Ἐγὼ γὰρ ἤδη σπένδομαι, καὶ ὁ καιρὸς τῆς ἀναλύσεώς μου **ἐφέστηκεν**. τὸν καλὸν ἀγῶνα **ἠγώνισμαι**, τὸν δρόμον **τετέλεκα**, τὴν πίστιν **τετήρηκα**.

*For I am already being poured out as a drink offering, and the time for my departure **has come**. I **have fought** the good fight, I **have finished** the race, I **have kept** the faith.*

These well-known verses witness Paul at the end of his apostolic ministry, speaking as though it is all over. But what if these perfect indicatives were not translated in the traditional manner? What if verbal aspect made it possible to translate these perfects more like present indicatives: the time *is coming; I am fighting* the good fight; *I am finishing* the race; *I am keeping* the faith? If this were a legitimate reading of the text, its meaning would be somewhat transformed.[3] Paul has not reached the end yet but

---

3. See Con Campbell, "Finished the Race? 2 Timothy 4:6–7 and Verbal Aspect," in *Donald Robinson Selected Works: Appreciation*, ed. Peter G. Bolt and Mark D. Thompson (Sydney: Australian Church Record/Moore College, 2008), 169–75.

is still actively engaged in his apostolic work. The study of verbal aspect opens up these kinds of exegetical possibilities that provide fresh insights into a number of texts.

Conclusion

Quite apart from all the exegetical possibilities it offers, the study of verbal aspect has brought some of the most significant developments in our understanding of ancient Greek over the last hundred years. In what follows, we will trace the history of research into verbal aspect in ancient Greek. We will look into linguistic theory and competing theoretical models. We will explore the aspectual constituency, meaning, and function of each tense-form across the moods, infinitive, and participle. We will aim to get verbal aspect right.

Part 1

Verbal Aspect Theory

Chapter 1

What is Verbal Aspect?

In this chapter, a definition of verbal aspect is offered and aspect is distinguished from two other important terms—tense and *Aktionsart*. Following this, the linguistic distinction between semantics and pragmatics is explained and is then applied to aspect, *Aktionsart*, and tense.

Verbal Aspect

While there are various ways of defining verbal aspect, the simplest description is *viewpoint*. An author or speaker views an action, event, or state either from the *outside* or from the *inside*. The view of an action, event, or state from the outside is called *perfective aspect*, while the view from the inside is called *imperfective aspect*. Buist Fanning describes aspect in this way:

> The action can be viewed from a reference-point *within* the action, without reference to the beginning or end-point of the action, but with a focus instead on its internal structure or make-up. Or the action can be viewed from a vantage-point *outside* the action, with focus on the whole action from beginning to end, but without reference to its internal structure.[1]

An illustration that has become standard in describing verbal aspect involves a reporter who is to report on a street parade.[2] If the reporter

---

1. Buist M. Fanning, *Verbal Aspect in New Testament Greek* (Oxford Theological Monographs; Oxford: Clarendon, 1990), 27.
2. The illustration originates with Isačenko and is adopted by Stanley Porter. See A. V. Isačenko, *Grammaticheskij stroj russkogo jazyka v sopostavlenii s slovatskim: Morfologija* (Bratislava: The Slovak Academy of Sciences Press, 1960); Stanley E. Porter, *Verbal Aspect in the Greek of the New Testament with Reference to Tense and Mood* (Studies in Biblical Greek 1; New York: Peter Lang, 1989), 91.

views the street parade from a helicopter, he sees the whole parade from a distance. He can describe the parade in a general way because he sees the whole thing rather than seeing its details up close. This viewpoint, from the helicopter, represents what we call *perfective aspect*. It is the view from the outside—the external viewpoint. If, however, that same reporter views the same street parade from the level of the street rather than from a helicopter, his view of the parade is quite different. This time the reporter is up close to the parade and watches as it unfolds before him. Rather than seeing the parade from a distance and as a whole, the parade is now seen from within. This viewpoint, from the street, represents what we call *imperfective aspect*. It is the view from the inside—the internal viewpoint.[3]

Most, if not all, languages have ways of expressing these two different viewpoints. In English, we can see the two viewpoints contrasted in the following sentences:

A. *I walked down the street. A man talked to me.*

B. *I was walking down the street when a man began talking to me.*

Both A and B might be describing the exact same events, but they nevertheless describe the events differently. The difference between them is verbal aspect. The actions portrayed in A are viewed as a whole; this is the view from the helicopter—perfective aspect. The same actions are portrayed in B as though unfolding; this is the view from the street—imperfective aspect.

Verbal aspect in Greek is called a *synthetic semantic category*. What this means is that aspect is realized in the morphological forms of verbs. In Greek, verbal aspect is encoded in the verb form of the verbal network. While this is not the same for all languages, most scholars agree that this is the case for Greek. This means that certain verbs encode certain aspects. For example, aorists express one aspect while presents express another. We'll look more closely at this later.

Verbal aspect represents a subjective choice. This point is important: aspect is, within certain bounds, subjective. An author chooses which aspect to use when portraying a particular action, event, or state. So, to take the examples from English mentioned above, to say *I was walking down the street when a man began talking to me* is no different in reality to *I walked down the street. A man talked to me.* In both cases, I walked down the street,

---

3. Strictly speaking, the reporter is not "within" the parade as he views it from the street. The point is that his view focuses on the inner features of the parade and does not include its beginning or end.

and a man talked to me. Both examples describe the same events. But each describes these events differently. When I'm telling the story, I decide which way I will tell it. Neither choice affects what really happened; the choice simply reflects my storytelling preference. This is what it means when we say that aspect represents a subjective choice.

Tense, *Aktionsart*, and Aspect

Verbal aspect is often discussed in relation to two other terms: tense and *Aktionsart*. It is important that careful delineation is made between the three terms.

Tense

In Greek, the verbs have traditionally been labeled as tenses. The aorist is a past tense, the present is a present tense, the future is a future tense, and so on. While there are more technical ways of defining tense, it normally refers to grammatical temporal reference. That is, referring to a particular time frame is the built-in meaning of a tense.

It doesn't take long when beginning to read the Greek New Testament, however, to discover that tense is not the whole story. We quickly discover present tense-form verbs that refer to the past. There are also forms traditionally considered as past tenses that refer to the present. There are even future-referring past tenses. Furthermore, what's the difference between two past tenses in Greek? Tense cannot be the whole story with Greek verbs, since there is a difference in meaning between the aorist and imperfect—both past tenses.[4] The nineteenth century answer to this question—the difference between two past tenses in Greek—is the type of action, or *Aktionsart*.

Aktionsart

This word is a German word that literally means "type of action." There are various types of action. There are punctiliar actions, iterative actions, ingressive actions, and so on. The category of *Aktionsart* describes how an action took place. If it happened as a once-occurring, instantaneous event, it is called punctiliar. If the action was repeated over and over, it is called iterative. If the action focuses on the beginning, it is called ingressive.

Early on in the academic discussion about such things, there was much confusion between *Aktionsart* and aspect. These days there is a general

---

4. Indeed, the same is true for English—tense is not the whole story, as the above English examples demonstrate.

consensus as to the difference between the two terms, and it is vital that we properly understand the distinction. *Aktionsart* refers to how an action actually takes place—what sort of action it is. Aspect refers to view-point—how the action is viewed. They are two different categories.

Let's take Romans 5:14 as an example. In that verse we are told that *Death reigned from the time of Adam to Moses.* The verb "reigned" expresses perfective aspect. This is the view from the helicopter. We are presented with a summary of what happened; we are told simply that it happened. This is the external viewpoint. But when we ask what *actually* happened, we are able to say a range of other things. For starters, this action took a long time! There were many years between Adam and Moses. Death's reign between Adam and Moses was an ongoing, expansive event. This was not a once-occurring, instantaneous type of action.

With this example, we can appreciate that there is a clear difference between aspect and *Aktionsart.* Aspect refers to how the action is viewed: it is viewed externally as a whole. *Aktionsart* refers to what actually happened: it was an ongoing event that spanned many years.

The difference between aspect and *Aktionsart* leads us to another important distinction.

Semantics and Pragmatics

The terms *semantics* and *pragmatics* come from modern linguistics and refer to a distinction that is now applied to the discussion about Greek verbs. Again, it is important that we understand what these terms mean.

Semantics

When speaking of verbs, *semantics* refers to the values that are encoded in the verbal form. These values are unchanging and are always there when the particular verbal form occurs (allowing for exceptional circumstances such as anomalous expressions and certain fixed idioms). In anything other than these exceptional circumstances, a semantic value is *uncancelable*—it is always there and cannot be canceled out. Semantics refers to what the verb means at its core. What does an aorist encode? What is core to an aorist that is different from an imperfect? What does an aorist *always* carry with it?

By the way, it is worth noting a little issue to do with terminology. Often the term *semantics* is used in a nontechnical sense to refer to the range of meaning that a word may have. This is not the sense in which it is now used in academic discussion. The range of meaning of a particular word is better termed *lexical semantics,* and the type of semantics that we are interested in at the moment is *verbal semantics* or *grammatical semantics*, which refers to the uncancelable properties of the verb form.

Pragmatics

When speaking of verbs, *pragmatics* refers to the expression of semantic values in context and in combination with other factors. In other words, pragmatics refers to how it all ends up—the way language is used in context.

The way that semantics and pragmatics relate together is a little like this: we take the semantic elements and plug them into a text that will have a range of things going on within it already, which bounce off and interact with the semantic values; the outcome is pragmatics. Pragmatic values can change from context to context; they are cancelable and not always there when particular verb forms are used.

Perhaps an illustration will help to clarify further the differences between semantics and pragmatics. Semantics asks, "Who am I?" while pragmatics asks, "What do I do?" These are two different questions (though our Western culture tends to blur them together). *Who I am* is about who I am at the core of my being—what it is that makes me uniquely me. Who I am might be expressed by what I do, but what I do is not who I am. If you were to ask me, "Who are you?" and I reply that I am a lawyer, I haven't really answered the question. Who am I? I'm Con. What do I do? I'm a lawyer. But I might quit law and take up jazz music. If I do that, I haven't changed who I am; I've just changed what I do (I know life's not quite as simple as that, but bear with the analogy). Discovering the semantics of the aorist is to ask, "Who are you, aorist?" To discover the pragmatics of the aorist, we ask, "And what do you do, aorist?"

The distinction between semantics and pragmatics is useful in sharpening the difference between aspect and *Aktionsart*. Aspect is a semantic value. The aspect of a particular tense-form doesn't change. An aorist will always be perfective in aspect. This will be the case no matter which word (lexeme) is used as an aorist or in what context it is used. Aspect is uncancelable. When asked, "Who are you, aorist?" the answer is, "I am perfective in aspect."

Aktionsart, on the other hand, is a pragmatic value. The *Aktionsart* of a particular tense-form can change. Sometimes an aorist will be punctiliar in *Aktionsart*. Sometimes it will be iterative, sometimes ingressive. It all depends on which lexeme is used as an aorist, on the context, and on what actually happened. *Aktionsart* is cancelable. When asked, "What do you do, aorist?" the answer is, "Well, I do many things. I have many possible

Aktionsart outcomes." Nearly all scholars working with Greek verbs now agree on this distinction between semantics and pragmatics.

The remaining question related to the distinction, however, is this: Is temporal reference semantic or pragmatic? If temporal reference is semantic, then Greek verbs truly are tenses. A verb's temporal reference is uncancelable and is a core part of its meaning. An aorist is a past tense and must always be a past tense.

But here, of course, lies a problem. We learn early on that aorists are *not* always past referring. Therefore, we are led to ask: Is past temporal reference a semantic value of the aorist? Some scholars say no, the aorist is not a past tense. Even though the aorist often ends up expressing past temporal reference when used in Greek texts, this is a *pragmatic implicature* rather than semantic encoding. After all, these scholars point out, there are plenty of other elements in the text that indicate what the time frame is to be understood as.

In fact, there are several languages in which the time frame is indicated purely by such *deictic markers*—words like "yesterday," "now," "later," and so forth. Even genre can set the time frame. For example, narratives naturally refer to the past (even without needing to use words like "yesterday") simply because it is understood that they are about events that have already happened. If the time frame is indicated by deictic markers and/or genre, why do we think that verbs must indicate time as well? The answer to that question, for most of us I think, is that we are used to that being the case in English (or so we think, anyway).[5]

But such is not the case in at least some other languages, and now the question has been raised with reference to the Greek verbal system. We will return to this issue at several points. Regardless of one's position on this matter, however, I think the term "tense-form" is more helpful than "tense" when referring to verbs, because it reminds us that it is the morphological *form* that is being addressed, whatever the form happens to communicate.

Conclusion

We have seen in this chapter that aspect refers to the viewpoint that an author subjectively chooses when portraying an action, event, or state. There are two viewpoints from which to choose: the view from the out-

---

5. In fact, English verbs are more complicated than most of us probably realize, and there is academic debate about its "tenses" too. Some scholars, for example, argue that the English present tense is not a tense at all, since it can refer to the present, past, and future.

side—perfective aspect—and the view from the inside—imperfective aspect. We have seen that aspect is different from *Aktionsart* in that the latter term describes how an action actually takes place, whereas aspect refers simply to viewpoint. Finally, we have seen that aspect is a semantic value encoded in the verb and is therefore uncancelable, whereas *Aktionsart* is a pragmatic value affected by a range of contextual factors and is therefore cancelable.

Chapter 2

The History of Verbal Aspect

Throughout the debate about verbal aspect in Ancient Greek, there has been not a little confusion created by the merging of three quite distinct academic disciplines: general linguistics, Greek philology, and New Testament research. In *general linguistics*, there are various linguistics schools, with their own terminology and methodological principles. It is from this sphere that terms such as *semantics*, *pragmatics*, and *implicature* come. *Greek philology* is the study of Ancient Greek generally. The corpus of literature written in Ancient Greek is huge and ranges from Homer, through classical Greek literature, right through to the New Testament and beyond. *New Testament research* has its own idiosyncrasies, but with reference to Greek is particularly interested in understanding for the sake of theological nuance, exegetical argument, and so forth. There is, of course, a strong focus on Koine Greek within this discipline.

Among the scholars who have engaged in debates about Greek verbal aspect, it is rare to find one who is equally comfortable on all three academic fronts. Most scholars have come from one, or at most two, of these three fields. Often scholars have been critical of those who have come from fields other than their own. Linguists sometimes claim that philologists are linguistically naïve; they may know the language well, but they lack the theoretical tools needed to analyze and describe it properly. Greek philologists tend to criticize New Testament scholars and particularly linguists for not knowing enough Greek. In their view, New Testament scholars are stuck in New Testament Koine, and linguists are just theorists interested in making generalizations without really knowing the language. Then again, New Testament scholars may defiantly declare that linguistics and classics both pale in comparison to God's Word!

It is no overstatement to claim that the study of Greek aspect has evolved through the significant contributions of all three academic fields, as we will now see.

The Early Period

Georg Curtius[1]

Georg Curtius was a nineteenth-century comparative philologist who was interested in Indo-European languages.[2] He made the first breakthrough with reference to the Greek verbal system. Curtis argued that in contrast to Latin, temporal meaning in the Greek verbal system was limited to the indicative mood. It is taken for granted now that there is no tense outside the indicative mood in Greek, but this was not formally acknowledged prior to Curtius.

A second major contribution of Curtius was to differentiate between distinct types of meaning expressed by the present and aorist verbal stems. He described this as a durative action as opposed to a "quickly-passing" action. His term for this distinction was called *Zeitart*, literally meaning "type of time." Curtius' type of time was different from a mere time lapse (short vs. long); he was interested in describing time in terms of a point versus a line. This description became standard and is still used today.

Curtius' insights were largely accepted in the late nineteenth century, and his analysis of the Greek verbal system became dominant. However, his term *Zeitart* was later replaced by the term *Aktionsart*, since "type of action" was regarded as being a more precise label than "type of time."

Curtius was aware of advances that had been made in the study of Slavonic languages, which predated his own discoveries, and through which the term *aspect* was introduced to the discussion.

Early Twentieth Century

Fanning describes the period of 1890–1910 as witnessing a flowering of aspect studies. Curtius had sparked a period of productive investigation into the nature of the Greek verbal system. Among the issues being investigated, an important question arose concerning the range of aspect values

---

1. Much of this section is reliant on Fanning, *Verbal Aspect*, 9–33.
2. Georg Curtius, *The Greek Verb: Its Structure and Development* (trans. Augustus S. Wilkins and Edwin B. England; London: John Murray, 1880).

that occur in Greek and Indo-European languages. The result of this, however, was that a multiplicity of categories was born, complete with conflicting terminology. Confusion resulted from the interchangeable usage of the three terms *Zeitart*, *Aktionsart*, and aspect.

In the mid-1920s attempts were made to definitively delineate between *Aktionsart* and aspect (*Zeitart* was dropped). The definitions that ensued were as follows: *Aktionsart* refers to how the action actually occurs and is primarily lexically determined; aspect refers to a way of viewing an action. This distinction is held today.

K.L. McKay

While there were several important contributions made through the middle of the twentieth century, such as those of J. Holt[3] and M. S. Ruipérez,[4] none had quite the same impact on the modern discussion as the work of K. L. McKay.[5] A Classical Greek philologist with an interest in the Greek of the New Testament, McKay first published on Greek aspect in 1965. In his 1965 article, McKay suggested that aspect was a more important feature of the Greek verbal system than was time.[6]

McKay posited that there were three or four aspects, depending on whether the future was regarded as a proper aspect. He viewed the present and imperfect tense-forms as imperfective in aspect, while the aorist was perfective (using our terminology). The future, though not actually an aspect, was labeled by McKay as a quasi-fourth aspect anyway. The perfect and pluperfect tense-forms were described as stative in aspect, a concept to be explored more fully later.

McKay wrote about aspect for the following thirty years and became progressively stronger in his assertions. In fact, he ended up saying that aspect is not just more important than time in the Greek verb, but that time is not there at all, except by implication from the verb's relationship to its context.[7] McKay's work did not gain wide acceptance for much of this period, but it is true to say that he had planted the seeds of the revolution.

---

3. Jens Holt, *Études d'aspect* (Acta Jutlandica Aarsskrift for Aarhus Universitet 15.2; Copenhagen: Munksgaard, 1943).

4. Martín S. Ruipérez, *Estructura del Sistema de Aspectos y Tiempos del Verbo Griego Antiguo: Análisis Funcional Sincrónico* (Theses et Studia Philologica Salmanticensia 7; Salamanca: Colegio Trilingüe de la Universidad, 1954).

5. K. L. McKay, *A New Syntax of the Verb in New Testament Greek: An Aspectual Approach* (Studies in Biblical Greek 5; New York: Peter Lang, 1994).

6. K. L. McKay, "The Use of the Ancient Greek Perfect Down to the Second Century A.D.," *Bulletin of the Institute of Classical Studies* 12 (1965): 1–21.

7. McKay, *Syntax of the Verb*, 39.

The Modern Period

It was the contributions of Stanley E. Porter[8] and Buist M. Fanning[9] that put verbal aspect firmly on the map again. Both men completed doctorates in England at the same time, which were published in 1989 and 1990 respectively. They were not aware of each other's simultaneous research, and it is therefore encouraging that there is a great deal of agreement between the two authors. There are, however, several strong differences, which have set the shape of the subsequent debate.

Stanley Porter

Porter is one of the few scholars who have been trained formally in both linguistics and theology. As such, he brings a robust theoretical linguistic framework to his analysis of the Greek verbal system. In particular, his analysis is conducted through the prism of the functional school of systemic linguistics. One important consequence of this is Porter's strong adherence to the distinction between semantics and pragmatics, which is essential to his analysis.

Porter self-consciously builds on the framework established by McKay. He too concludes that Greek is aspectual and not tense-based at all. But unlike McKay, Porter rigorously defends this view from a theoretical basis. Since temporal reference is not always expressed by the verb, it therefore cannot be a semantic value. Temporal reference must be pragmatic.

Porter also acknowledges three aspects in the Greek verbal system: perfective, imperfective, and stative. The future is nonaspectual according to his analysis.

It is Porter's contribution that has caused the fiercest debate. The "tenseless" position is still very much in the minority, being rejected by most traditionalists.

Buist Fanning

Fanning's analysis is more traditional than Porter's. For him, while aspect is regarded as being dominant, tense is still a legitimate category. The aorist is still to be regarded as a past tense and the present as a present tense, and so on, but the dominance of aspect over tense provides explanation of those cases in which the temporal expression is not consistent. According

---

8. Stanley E. Porter, *Verbal Aspect in the Greek of the New Testament with Reference to Tense and Mood* (Studies in Biblical Greek 1; New York: Peter Lang, 1989).

9. Buist M. Fanning, *Verbal Aspect in New Testament Greek* (Oxford Theological Monographs; Oxford: Clarendon, 1990).

to Fanning, there are only two aspects, not three, since stativity is properly regarded as an *Aktionsart* category rather than an aspect.

Fanning provides a detailed analysis of how aspect relates to *Aktionsart*, indicating how each aspect interacts with certain lexical types to produce predictable *Aktionsart* outcomes. His work has been more readily accepted by traditionalists, provoking considerably less controversy than Porter, but it may not be as well respected among theoretical linguists because it is less rigorously linguistic in framework and methodology.

Mari Broman Olsen

Olsen is the first major contributor to follow Porter and Fanning, and her work reflects the enormous debt that the modern discussion owes them.[10] Her contribution is very much on the linguistic side of things, with one chapter on English aspect, one chapter specifically on Koine Greek aspect, and the remainder providing a detailed study of theoretical issues.

Olsen defines aspect a little differently, as "internal temporal constituency," following Comrie and others. This is not quite the same thing as defining aspect simply as viewpoint, and as such it yields somewhat different results. Like Fanning, Olsen advocates only two aspects, again affirming that stativity is an *Aktionsart* value rather than being aspectual.

Interestingly, Olsen utilizes the semantic/pragmatic distinction to argue that some Greek verb forms are tenses and others are not. This is simply a matter of which forms are consistent in their temporal reference and which are not. Those that are consistent encode temporal reference at the semantic level and those that are not consistent do not encode temporal reference at the semantic level.

In terms of the reception of Olsen's work, it is not as well known within New Testament circles as it deserves to be, and this is probably due in part to its highly technical nature. The work is linguistically rigorous, which means that it is somewhat inaccessible to the uninitiated.

Rodney J. Decker

Decker comes from the New Testament scholarship stable. The burden of his work is to test Porter's nontense position.[11] He admits that he began his investigations into aspect somewhat skeptical towards Porter's approach, but later accepted its validity.

---

10. Mari Broman Olsen, *A Semantic and Pragmatic Model of Lexical and Grammatical Aspect* (Outstanding Dissertations in Linguistics; New York: Garland, 1997).

11. Rodney J. Decker, *Temporal Deixis of the Greek Verb in the Gospel of Mark with Reference to Verbal Aspect* (Studies in Biblical Greek 10; New York: Peter Lang, 2001).

A unique feature of Decker's work is the source limitation imposed within it, focusing on Mark's Gospel. The strength of this method is that it allows for thorough testing, whereas some other studies had been too broad in their sample. This also limits the comprehensiveness of the results; what does it say about the rest of the New Testament? What about Greek more widely?

Decker has made a significant contribution to the discussion by isolating one particular issue—the existence or otherwise of semantic temporal reference—and investigating that question thoroughly. As for the reception of his work, classicists tend to overlook it, probably due to its limited scope. As for New Testament students, however, Decker explains Porter's approach in an accessible manner, and the testing of the controversial issue of temporal reference is of great value.

T. V. Evans

Evans is a classical philologist who seeks to respect linguistic considerations and the input of New Testament scholarship.[12] Because of his classicist background, he brings a broader knowledge of Greek literature to the discussion, having done extensive work on aspect in classical texts and the Septuagint.

On the temporality issue, Evans is a traditionalist, arguing that tense is indeed expressed by the verbal system. On the question of aspects, he also affirms the existence of two aspects, rejecting the category of stative aspect.

In terms of the reception of Evans' work, it is well regarded within classical scholarship, and there are signs that it is being noticed within New Testament circles.

Constantine R. Campbell

I have approached verbal aspect through New Testament studies. My first book deals with verbal aspect in the indicative mood and its role in narrative texts.[13] Wanting to gain the benefits of a limited sample (following Decker) and yet also attempting to minimize the trade-off of such an approach, I investigated a couple of New Testament narrative texts as well as a series of nonbiblical texts. My second book looks at verbal aspect in the nonindicative verbs.[14]

---

12. T. V. Evans, *Verbal Syntax in the Greek Pentateuch: Natural Greek Usage and Hebrew Interference* (Oxford: Oxford Univ. Press, 2001).

13. Constantine R. Campbell, *Verbal Aspect, the Indicative Mood, and Narrative: Soundings in the Greek of the New Testament* (Studies in Biblical Greek 13; New York: Peter Lang, 2007).

14. Constantine R. Campbell, *Verbal Aspect and Non-Indicative Verbs: Further Soundings in the Greek of the New Testament* (Studies in Biblical Greek 15; New York: Peter Lang, 2008).

I follow Porter and Decker on the issue of tense: it is not regarded as a semantic value of verbs in the indicative mood, even though each tense-form has a characteristic temporal reference on the pragmatic level. I argue that there are only two aspects, rejecting the category of stative aspect. Perhaps most controversially, I mount the argument that the perfect and pluperfect tense-forms are imperfective in aspect.

Current Issues

Areas of Agreement

There are several areas of agreement within current debate about Greek verbal aspect. Perhaps the most important among these is the common assent that aspect is a major category in our understanding of Greek. It is more important than tense and must be reckoned with. There are other areas of agreement as well:

- Aspect holds the key to understanding the Greek verbal system.
- There are at least two aspects in Greek: perfective and imperfective.
- Debate about aspect must come to some kind of resolution as quickly as possible.
- Greek grammars and New Testament commentaries need to update and come to grips with the new playing field.
- Responsible exegesis of the Greek text must incorporate aspectual sensitivity.

Unresolved Areas

Nevertheless, there are a few areas that are as yet unresolved.

Temporality and tense. The issue of whether or not Greek verbs are tenses remains unresolved. Do Greek verbs encode temporal reference at the semantic level? The nontense position is still in the minority across those who teach and learn ancient Greek. Nevertheless, it is worth noting that among the major contributors in the modern debate, the nontense position is slightly dominant.

Number of aspects. The issue of how many aspects are encoded in the Greek verbal system is of enormous importance and is also as yet unresolved. Are there two aspects, or three (or four)? Certainly there are perfective and imperfective aspects, but what about stative aspect? Generally speaking, among those who teach and learn ancient Greek, most seem to accept the existence of three aspects. But the major contributors to the modern debate clearly prefer the two-aspect position, rejecting stative aspect. Indeed, within the wider linguistic world, two aspects are standard across languages. To regard stativity as an aspect is quite odd.

The Way Forward

In order to reach some kind of consensus on these issues, there is a range of approaches that will aid the discussion.

1. Methodological issues need to be sharpened and clarified.
2. There needs to be a greater sensitivity displayed between the three academic disciplines involved in the debate (general linguistics, Greek philology, and New Testament research). All three spheres should listen to each other with respect.
3. The power of explanation needs to be appreciated as a key methodological principle. We must seek the model with the greatest power of explanation. Is a particular model of the verbal system able to account for all uses of the verb?
4. We must uncover the relationship of aspect to discourse analysis, but more on this later.

Chapter 3

Perfective Aspect

———

Perfective aspect is the external viewpoint, with which an author portrays an action, event, or state from the outside. Perfective aspect is like a reporter who describes a street parade from a helicopter. It provides an all-encompassing, or summary, view of an action. From the view in the helicopter, the street parade is seen at a distance, and the details of the parade are not appreciated. Exactly how the parade is unfolding is not seen.

The Aorist Tense-Form

The aorist tense-form is universally regarded as being perfective in aspect. This means that the aorist provides an external view of an action. It presents events in summary, from a distance and does not view the details of how the action took place. An example from Matthew 4 demonstrates this well.

> **Matthew 4:21–22** καὶ προβὰς ἐκεῖθεν **εἶδεν** ἄλλους δύο ἀδελφούς, Ἰάκωβον τὸν τοῦ Ζεβεδαίου καὶ Ἰωάννην τὸν ἀδελφὸν αὐτοῦ, ἐν τῷ πλοίῳ μετὰ Ζεβεδαίου τοῦ πατρὸς αὐτῶν καταρτίζοντας τὰ δίκτυα αὐτῶν, καὶ **ἐκάλεσεν** αὐτούς. οἱ δὲ εὐθέως ἀφέντες τὸ πλοῖον καὶ τὸν πατέρα αὐτῶν **ἠκολούθησαν** αὐτῷ.

> *And going on from there **he saw** two other brothers, James the son of Zebedee and John his brother, in the boat with Zebedee their father, mending their nets, and **he called** them. Immediately they left the boat and their father and **followed** him.*

We see here that the main actions in this little extract are communicated through the use of aorist indicatives: "he saw ... he called ... they followed." These aorists are not used for presenting the details of what happened. The content of what Jesus saw is provided through a participial clause. We are not told what Jesus said when he called them. We are not told about James and John's thoughts in response to Jesus. We are not told whether or not they spoke to their father as they left him in the boat. We are told, quite simply, that they followed Jesus, and that's that.

It is worth mentioning that just because an action is presented in summary does not necessarily mean that the action is unimportant. To think this way would be to make a category error. No, some actions that are presented in summary, and indeed as aorists, are tremendously important.

Furthermore, aorists may portray actions that in reality took a long time taking place. Just because the action is presented in summary does not mean that it happened quickly. Take Romans 5:14, for example:

Romans 5:14 ἀλλὰ **ἐβασίλευσεν** ὁ θάνατος ἀπὸ Ἀδὰμ μέχρι Μωϋσέως.

*But death **reigned** from the time of Adam to Moses.*

The period of time set by the phrase "from the time of Adam to Moses" indicates that death's reign occurred over a long interval. There are many years during which this event took place. This example demonstrates that the use of the aorist does not indicate that an action occurred in an instant. Rather, the event is simply viewed from a distance in summary.

Thus, it is important to dispel an old myth about the aorist. The term "punctiliar aorist" is a common one and refers to a legitimate use of the aorist. Unfortunately, some scholars have mistakenly concluded that the term "punctiliar" describes the aorist tense-form in general. They think that the aorist *always* depicts a punctiliar, once-occurring, instantaneous action. The aorist in Romans 5:6 is sometimes treated this way.

Romans 5:6 Ἔτι γὰρ Χριστὸς ὄντων ἡμῶν ἀσθενῶν ἔτι κατὰ καιρὸν ὑπὲρ ἀσεβῶν **ἀπέθανεν**.

*For while we were still weak, at the right time Christ **died** for the ungodly.*

Some commentators write that because an aorist is used here, Romans 5:6 proves that Christ's death was a once-occurring event, never to be repeated, and therefore Christ could not be reoffered time and time again in the Roman mass. While not wanting to deny the once-for-all nature of

Christ's death (cf. 1 Peter 3:18), the aorist in Romans 5:6 does not prove the point at all. If we look ahead a few verses, we come to 5:14 (see above), where we see an aorist that plainly depicts death reigning from the time of Adam to Moses. To reiterate, this is not a once-for-all action. It is not punctiliar.

Confusion about the so-called punctiliar aorist has no doubt arisen from the fact that the aorist presents an action in summary. A street parade may look like a dot when you're looking at it from a helicopter high in the sky, but that does not mean that the parade actually is a dot. Just because an action is viewed in summary through use of an aorist does not mean that it occurred like a dot. The use of the aorist does not mean that an action is once-occurring just because it is conveyed with perfective aspect. It must be remembered that aspect is viewpoint. Perfective aspect refers to the viewpoint from which the action is viewed; it says nothing about how the action actually occurred.

Tense?

An important issue to consider is whether or not the aorist tense-form is a past tense. The traditional answer to this question is, of course, "yes." There are, however, many problematic instances. Mark 1:11 provides us with a famous example.

> **Mark 1:11** καὶ φωνὴ ἐγένετο ἐκ τῶν οὐρανῶν· σὺ εἶ ὁ υἱός μου ὁ ἀγαπητός, ἐν σοὶ **εὐδόκησα**.
>
> *And a voice came from heaven, "You are my beloved Son; in you I am well pleased."*

Suffice to say that *no one* translates the last clause of this verse, *"in you I was well pleased."* It simply doesn't fit the theological or literary context to read the aorist that way. There are many such instances within the usage of the aorist where this so-called past tense is obviously not past referring.

To recall the discussion in the first chapter, if we take seriously the distinction between semantics and pragmatics, we are forced to ask how past temporal reference can be a semantic value of the aorist. In fact, only about eighty-five percent of aorist indicatives refer to the past in New Testament usage.[1] Theoretically, if past temporal reference were a semantic value, we

---

1. D. A. Carson, "An Introduction to the Porter/Fanning Debate," in *Biblical Greek Language and Linguistics: Open Questions in Current Research*, ed. Stanley E. Porter and D. A. Carson (JSNTSup 80; Sheffield: Sheffield Academic Press, 1993), 25.

would expect the aorist to refer to the past in every instance (or something close to that, allowing for the humanity of language use). Because of the importance of the semantic/pragmatic distinction, past temporal reference is not here regarded as a semantic value of the aorist. If, however, the aorist is not a past tense, then what is it?

Remoteness

Traditionally, the aorist tense-form has been regarded as perfective in aspect and past in tense. If we do not accept the tense part of that equation, the aorist tense-form is perfective in aspect and ... what? Some scholars have argued that *remoteness* is a better description of the semantics of the aorist tense-form, alongside perfective aspect.[2]

Remoteness refers to the metaphorical value of distance. This fits nicely with perfective aspect, in the way we have already described the perfective aspect as the view "from afar." It goes hand in hand with viewing the parade from the helicopter; the view is a summary view precisely because the parade is viewed from a distance.

Remoteness is regarded as a semantic value—it is always there when the aorist tense-form is used. But it has a range of pragmatic functions. It may not be a surprise to learn that the major pragmatic function that remoteness effects is past temporal reference. In fact, the semantic value of remoteness will be pragmatically expressed as past temporal reference approximately eighty-five percent of the time. An event that is in the past is naturally remote—temporally remote. Thus, past temporal reference is still regarded as one of the major uses of the aorist tense-form, but it is understood as a pragmatic expression of the aorist rather than as part of its semantic meaning.

Remoteness also offers explanation for those fifteen percent of aorists that do not refer to the past. Such aorists may refer to the present or even to the future, but they would still be regarded as remote. The difference with these cases is that the remoteness is not temporal remoteness. There are other kinds of remoteness besides temporal remoteness, such as logical remoteness.

To return to the example above from Mark 1:11, remoteness offers the key to understanding the aorist εὐδόκησα. The semantic value of remoteness that is encoded in the aorist indicative does not in this instance function to provide past temporal reference. Instead, remoteness functions

---

2. Along with this, it has been suggested that the augment is a morphological marker of remoteness rather than a marker of past temporal reference, as traditional analyses describe it. For an overview, see Campbell, *Indicative Mood*, 88–91.

together with perfective aspect to provide a bird's-eye view of the scene. As the Father speaks from heaven, he gives his assessment of his Son—he is well pleased. Certain things in the context indicate that this assessment comes from heaven itself and breaks into the earthly scene. We are told that the heavens were *torn open*, and that the Spirit *descended* like a dove (v.10). The effect of these elements is that the "verdict" of heaven upon Jesus is being delivered *from heaven to earth*, as it were.

This "verdict" is not given with reference to any particular action but refers to Jesus—his person and works—as a whole. As such, there could not be a more appropriate choice of tense-form here. The aorist offers a summary view, because of perfective aspect, and because Jesus' life is viewed from afar. This does not imply that the Father is relationally *distant* from the Son, or some such viewpoint, but that on this occasion he views his Son from afar in order to view the whole. God may not be in a helicopter (!), but this scene enables a vantage-point that provides a somewhat similar view as from a helicopter—from heaven above itself.

Narrative Function

As a remote perfective tense-form, the aorist indicative plays an important role in narrative texts. Because the aorist indicative provides a bird's-eye view of an action (or a helicopter view) and portrays actions in summary, it is often used to outline the skeletal structure of a narrative. The basic outline of events in the story is presented by the aorist in quick succession: Jesus went ... this happened ... Jesus said ... and so on. This basic outline, or skeletal structure, is called the mainline of a narrative. Consider the following passage.

> **Matthew 8:32–34** καὶ **εἶπεν** αὐτοῖς ... οἱ δὲ ... **ἀπῆλθον** ...
> **ὥρμησεν** πᾶσα ἡ ἀγέλη ... **ἀπέθανον** ... οἱ δὲ βόσκοντες **ἔφυγον** ...
> **ἀπήγγειλαν** ... πᾶσα ἡ πόλις **ἐξῆλθεν** ... **παρεκάλεσαν**...
>
> *He (Jesus) said to them ... and they (evil spirits) departed ... the whole herd rushed ... they died ... the herdsmen fled ... they announced ... the whole town came out ... they begged...*

In just three short verses, a huge amount of action is portrayed. The story moves from Jesus casting out the evil spirits right through to the town casting out Jesus. The passage is fast, compressed, and covers a lot of ground. Such is the effect of the narrative aorist.

Narratives usually provide more information besides the skeletal outline of events, but such details are typically conveyed by other tense-forms. The basic actions are normally aorists, and this fact helps us to recognize the elemental structure of narratives. It is important to note, however, that this narrative function is pragmatic; it is a function that the aorist has within narrative, arising from its semantic nature. Aorists are often found performing different roles within narrative texts, and other tense-forms may be found outlining the narrative mainline, but this is of no concern, since we are talking about pragmatics, which are variable and cancelable.

The Future Tense-Form

Verbal aspect in the future tense-form is an unresolved issue within academic discussion. Some scholars have suggested that the future is nonaspectual, while others say it is perfective in aspect, and yet others say that it is a combination of perfective and imperfective. We will not explore the relevant issues here, though part of the difficulty assessing such things with the future tense-form no doubt arises from the problems related to speaking of events that are future. I have argued elsewhere that the future tense-form is perfective in aspect, and that position is adopted here.[3]

Furthermore, the future tense-form is a real tense. That is, future temporal reference is a semantic feature of the form. This is easily derived by the fact that all futures refer to the future. There are no past-referring futures; there are no present-referring futures. The future always refers to the future.

Thus, the semantic values of the future indicative tense-form are perfective aspect and future temporal reference. Remoteness is not a separate semantic feature of the future tense-form, though it should be clear that future temporal reference is naturally remote, but this is simply an outcome of future temporal reference rather than the other way around.

In this way, the aorist and future tense-forms are closely related, and yet distinct. They both share perfective aspect, but the former also semantically encodes the spatial value of remoteness, while the latter also semantically encodes future temporal reference.

---

3. See Campbell, *Indicative Mood*, 127–60.

Chapter 4

Imperfective Aspect

—‿‿—

Imperfective aspect provides the view from the inside—an action is presented as though unfolding before the eyes. This is the view of the parade from the street, as the parade goes by, rather than the view from the helicopter. The effect of the street view is that we watch the action unfold. While we may not see the beginning or end of the parade because they're out of view, we are able to appreciate the details of how the parade unfolds.

The Present Tense-Form

The present tense-form is universally regarded as being imperfective in aspect. This means that the present portrays actions with a view from the inside; we watch as the action unfolds before our eyes. This is easy to appreciate in English: *"he is walking down the street"* is clearly cast before us as though we are watching it happen. The following passage provides a good example in Greek.

> **Mark 4:14–20** ὁ σπείρων τὸν λόγον **σπείρει**. οὗτοι δέ **εἰσιν** οἱ παρὰ τὴν ὁδόν· ὅπου **σπείρεται** ὁ λόγος καὶ ὅταν ἀκούσωσιν, εὐθὺς **ἔρχεται** ὁ σατανᾶς καὶ **αἴρει** τὸν λόγον τὸν ἐσπαρμένον εἰς αὐτούς. καὶ οὗτοί **εἰσιν** οἱ ἐπὶ τὰ πετρώδη σπειρόμενοι, οἳ ὅταν ἀκούσωσιν τὸν λόγον εὐθὺς μετὰ χαρᾶς **λαμβάνουσιν** αὐτόν, καὶ οὐκ **ἔχουσιν** ῥίζαν ἐν ἑαυτοῖς ἀλλὰ πρόσκαιροί **εἰσιν**, εἶτα γενομένης θλίψεως ἢ διωγμοῦ διὰ τὸν λόγον εὐθὺς **σκανδαλίζονται**. καὶ ἄλλοι **εἰσιν** οἱ εἰς τὰς ἀκάνθας σπειρόμενοι· οὗτοί **εἰσιν** οἱ τὸν λόγον ἀκούσαντες, καὶ αἱ μέριμναι τοῦ αἰῶνος καὶ ἡ ἀπάτη τοῦ πλούτου καὶ αἱ περὶ τὰ λοιπὰ ἐπιθυμίαι

εἰσπορευόμεναι **συμπνίγουσιν** τὸν λόγον καὶ ἄκαρπος **γίνεται**. καὶ ἐκεῖνοί **εἰσιν** οἱ ἐπὶ τὴν γῆν τὴν καλὴν σπαρέντες, οἵτινες **ἀκούουσιν** τὸν λόγον καὶ **παραδέχονται** καὶ **καρποφοροῦσιν** ἐν τριάκοντα καὶ ἐν ἑξήκοντα καὶ ἐν ἑκατόν.

*The sower **sows** the word. And these **are** the ones along the path, where the word **is sown**: when they hear, Satan immediately **comes** and **takes** away the word that is sown in them. And these **are** the ones sown on rocky ground: the ones who, when they hear the word, immediately **receive** it with joy. And **they have** no root in themselves, but **are** only temporary. Then, when tribulation or persecution arises on account of the word, immediately **they fall away**. And others **are** the ones sown among thorns. They **are** those who hear the word, but the cares of the world and the deceitfulness of riches and the desires for other things enter in and **choke** the word, and it **becomes** unfruitful. But those **are** the ones that **were** sown on the good soil, who **hear** the word and **accept it** and **bear fruit**, thirtyfold and sixtyfold and a hundredfold.*

In this passage, Jesus explains the parable of the sower by laying out its meaning before the disciples' eyes. It is interesting to note that the actual parable, told in 4:3–8, is conveyed with aorist indicatives rather than presents. This is not surprising, since a parable is a little embedded narrative, which is a natural setting for aorists. But here, as Jesus explains what the story means, it is as though he is opening the story out. By explaining what the story means, Jesus turns his original story into general teaching: this is what happens when the word is sown...

Proximity

The present is not the only tense-form that is regarded as being imperfective in aspect. The imperfect tense-form is also universally regarded as imperfective. The question must be raised, therefore, as to how these two imperfective tense-forms are to be distinguished from each other. Traditionally, the distinguishing factor between the present and imperfect tense-forms was understood to be tense. The imperfect is a past tense, and the present is a present tense.

Consistent with the spatial approach adopted so far, however, we note that Porter has suggested that the distinguishing factor is remoteness. The imperfect is imperfective and remote, while the present is imperfective and nonremote. I have argued elsewhere that nonremoteness, which is absence of remoteness, should be replaced by *proximity*. Proximity is not simply the absence of remoteness, but is a positive value of its own, which is opposite to remoteness. As such, I regard the imperfect tense-form to be imperfective in aspect, with the spatial value of remoteness, while the present tense-form is imperfective in aspect, with the spatial value of proximity. This may be illustrated by the following diagrams.

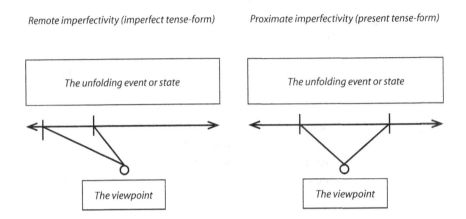

Remote imperfectivity (imperfect tense-form)   *Proximate imperfectivity (present tense-form)*

Imagine that these diagrams represent the imperfective view of the reporter on the street. The second diagram—imperfective aspect and proximity—depicts the view of the street parade directly in front of the reporter. He not only views the parade unfolding before his eyes, but is viewing that part of the parade that is directly in front of him, to which he is closest. On the other hand, the first diagram—imperfective aspect and remoteness—depicts the view of the street parade as he looks down the street a little. As he views the parade unfolding before his eyes, he is not viewing the part of the parade directly in front of him, but is looking further down the parade. This part of the parade is not so close, even though he still sees it unfolding.

Narrative Function

In narrative texts, the present tense-form is most often found in discourse—direct, indirect, or authorial discourse. This fact fits with the semantic analysis of the present given above, since discourse creates an imperfective proximate context. What this means is that whenever discourse is portrayed in narrative, it has the effect of drawing the readers into the story, as the discourse is presented before their eyes. It is as though we are seeing the events unfold before us. As such, discourse inherently forms an imperfective context (we see it unfold), and a proximate context (it is as though we are right there).

This is why the present tense-form is so well suited to discourse: it is an imperfective proximate tense-form that fits naturally within an imperfective proximate context. This is not the only function of the present tense-form, but it is one of the major pragmatic functions within narrative literature. One notable nondiscourse use of the present tense-form is the so-called historical present, to which we now turn.

The Historical Present

This term refers to the common phenomenon of present tense-forms that refer to the past. In the New Testament, historical presents are particularly common in Mark and John. There are two types of historical presents, stemming from two distinct groups of lexemes used with the present. The first group of lexemes that are used as historical presents are *verbs of propulsion*. These are verbs of coming and going, giving and taking, raising up and putting down, and so forth. Basically, these are verbs where there is some kind of propulsion from one point to another.

The second group of lexemes consists of verbs that introduce discourse. There are verbs of speaking, thinking, writing, and so on, which typically segue into speech, thought, and other types of discourse. While historical presents will be explored again in chapter 7, we see both types of historical present in the following passage.

> **John 8:3–4** Ἄγουσιν δὲ οἱ γραμματεῖς καὶ οἱ Φαρισαῖοι γυναῖκα ἐπὶ μοιχείᾳ κατειλημμένην καὶ στήσαντες αὐτὴν ἐν μέσῳ **λέγουσιν** αὐτῷ· διδάσκαλε, αὕτη ἡ γυνὴ κατείληπται ἐπ᾽ αὐτοφώρῳ μοιχευομένη.
>
> *The scribes and the Pharisees **brought** a woman who had been caught in adultery, and placing her in the midst **they said** to him, "Teacher, this woman has been caught in the act of adultery."*

The verb ἄγουσιν is a verb of propulsion, while λέγουσιν introduces the direct discourse that follows. While this will be unpacked a little more later, the semantic description of the present tense-form as imperfective in aspect with the spatial value of proximity provides the best explanation as to why these lexemes are used with the historical present.

The Imperfect Tense-Form

As mentioned above, the imperfect tense-form is imperfective in aspect with the spatial value of remoteness. In this way, the imperfect shares semantic values with both the present and aorist tense-forms. It shares imperfective aspect with the present tense-form, and it shares remoteness with the aorist tense-form.

The sharing of remoteness with the aorist means that the imperfect is also found in narrative proper rather than discourse. While aorists provide the skeletal structure of narrative proper, imperfects tend to provide supplemental information. This supplemental information contributes to narrative by giving information beyond the narrative mainline; it describes, explains, and provides background; it puts flesh on the skeleton. This key function of the imperfect tense-form is a pragmatic feature and is therefore cancelable.

This supplemental function of the imperfect fits with its semantic meaning. Background and supplemental information naturally creates a remote context, since it supplements the remote narrative mainline. While mainline is naturally remote, it is also naturally perfective; events are presented in summary outline. In contrast, supplemental information is off the mainline—and is properly called *offline*—and presents information from the inside because it describes details, provides reasons and explanations, and elucidates motivations, all of which would not be seen through the summary external view. We may observe the complementary narrative functions of aorists and imperfects in the following example, in which the aorist indicatives are boldface and the imperfects are bold and underlined.

Luke 9:42–45 ἔτι δὲ προσερχομένου αὐτοῦ **ἔρρηξεν** αὐτὸν τὸ δαιμόνιον καὶ **συνεσπάραξεν· ἐπετίμησεν** δὲ ὁ Ἰησοῦς τῷ πνεύματι τῷ ἀκαθάρτῳ καὶ **ἰάσατο** τὸν παῖδα καὶ **ἀπέδωκεν** αὐτὸν τῷ πατρὶ αὐτοῦ. **<u>ἐξεπλήσσοντο</u>** δὲ πάντες ἐπὶ τῇ μεγαλειότητι τοῦ θεοῦ. Πάντων δὲ θαυμαζόντων ἐπὶ πᾶσιν οἷς **<u>ἐποίει</u> εἶπεν** πρὸς τοὺς μαθητὰς αὐτοῦ· θέσθε ὑμεῖς εἰς τὰ ὦτα ὑμῶν τοὺς λόγους τούτους· ὁ γὰρ υἱὸς τοῦ ἀνθρώπου μέλλει παραδίδοσθαι εἰς χεῖρας ἀνθρώπων. οἱ δὲ **<u>ἠγνόουν</u>** τὸ ῥῆμα τοῦτο καὶ ἦν παρακεκαλυμμένον ἀπ᾽ αὐτῶν ἵνα μὴ αἴσθωνται αὐτό, καὶ **<u>ἐφοβοῦντο</u>** ἐρωτῆσαι αὐτὸν περὶ τοῦ ῥήματος τούτου.

While he was coming, the demon **threw** *him to the ground and* **convulsed** *him. But Jesus* **rebuked** *the unclean spirit and* **healed** *the boy, and* **gave** *him back to his father. And all* **<u>were astonished</u>** *at the majesty of God. But while they were all marveling at everything he* **<u>was doing</u>**, *Jesus* **said** *to his disciples, "Let these words sink into your ears: The Son of Man is about to be delivered into the hands of men." But* **<u>they did not understand</u>** *this saying, and it was concealed from them, so that they might not perceive it. And* **<u>they were afraid</u>** *to ask him about this saying.*

Notice here that the mainline is carried by the aorists *threw, convulsed, rebuked, healed, gave,* and *said*; these verbs convey the sequence of events in the narrative. However, the imperfects *astonished, not understand,* and *afraid* do not convey mainline action, rather they provide supplementary material. We are told of the disciples' reactions to the actions that have taken place and to Jesus' words, and that they are afraid to ask him about his saying. This information does not contribute to the mainline of the narrative, but rather gives the reader an inside view into the thought-world of the disciples.

Chapter 5

The Problem of the Perfect

---—*∿∿*—---

The semantic nature of the perfect and pluperfect tense-forms is one of the great puzzles in Greek linguistics. There are several suggested options, ranging from the traditional analysis, to perfective aspect, stative aspect, and imperfective aspect. In this chapter we will briefly canvas most of these options before concluding that the perfect is imperfective in aspect.

The Perfect Tense-Form

Traditionally the perfect tense-form was understood as indicating a past action with ongoing consequences. To use the *Aktionsart* descriptions of an earlier period, the perfect was like a dot and a line. In this way, the perfect was almost a combination of aorist and present tenses—an aoristic action followed by a present state. The great problem with this analysis is that it doesn't work. It yields far too many exceptions, reflected in the multiplicity of categories of perfects listed by grammars. The following examples illustrate the problem.

Many perfects don't express a past action, but only envisage the ongoing consequences:

> **John 1:26** ἀπεκρίθη αὐτοῖς ὁ Ἰωάννης λέγων· ἐγὼ βαπτίζω ἐν ὕδατι· μέσος ὑμῶν **ἕστηκεν** ὃν ὑμεῖς οὐκ **οἴδατε**.
>
> *John answered them, "I baptize with water, but among you **stands** one you do not **know**."*

Another example are those perfects that don't express any ongoing consequences, but only the past action:

Revelation 8:5 καὶ **εἴληφεν** ὁ ἄγγελος τὸν λιβανωτὸν καὶ ἐγέμισεν αὐτόν.

*Then the angel **took** the censer and filled it.*

These examples provide just two of the symptoms that indicate the problems faced by the traditional explanation of the perfect. See the grammars for variations on this theme.

Unfortunately, verbal aspect has not so quickly resolved the matter. We will now briefly survey the attempts that have been made to analyze the perfect in terms of aspect.

Stative Aspect

An aspect not mentioned before this point is called stative aspect. According to McKay, stative aspect views the state, or state of being, of the subject of a verb.[1]

Luke 20:21 καὶ ἐπηρώτησαν αὐτὸν λέγοντες· διδάσκαλε, **οἴδαμεν** ὅτι ὀρθῶς λέγεις καὶ διδάσκεις καὶ οὐ λαμβάνεις πρόσωπον, ἀλλ᾽ ἐπ᾽ ἀληθείας τὴν ὁδὸν τοῦ θεοῦ διδάσκεις.

*So they asked him, "Teacher, **we know** that you speak and teach rightly, and show no partiality, but truly teach the way of God."*

By McKay's approach, this perfect is indicating that the disciples ("we") are in a state of knowing that Jesus speaks and teaches rightly. The force of the perfect is to communicate that they are in this state of knowing. So far so good.

Problems start to arise for McKay's conception of the perfect, however, with cases where it seems difficult to attribute the state to the subject rather than the object of the verb. This problem has plagued traditional analyses of the perfect also, but whereas Wackernagel suggested that the stativity should be understood as applying to the object of the verb (i.e., the resultative perfect),[2] McKay suggests something else. He is right to insist that we cannot just transfer the meaning of the perfect onto the object of

---

1. McKay, *Syntax of the Verb*, 31.

2. Jakob Wackernagel, "Studien zum griechischen Perfectum," in *Programm zur akademischen Preisverteilung* (n.p., 1904), 3–24. Repr., idem, *Kleine Schriften* (Göttingen: Vandenhoeck und Ruprecht, 1953), 1000–1021.

the verb, and the apparent need to do so flags a problem with our understanding of the perfect. In such cases, McKay argues that the subject is to be seen as *the one responsible for the action.*[3] This appears to work in many cases, but there are some significantly problematic cases also, such as we see in the example below.

> **John 7:22** διὰ τοῦτο Μωϋσῆς **δέδωκεν** ὑμῖν τὴν περιτομήν – οὐχ ὅτι ἐκ τοῦ Μωϋσέως ἐστὶν ἀλλ᾽ ἐκ τῶν πατέρων – καὶ ἐν σαββάτῳ περιτέμνετε ἄνθρωπον.
>
> *Moses **gave** you circumcision (not that it is from Moses, but from the fathers), and you circumcise a man upon the Sabbath.*

This is a good example demonstrating that it is not the responsibility of the subject in view here. According to McKay's approach, Moses as the subject must be viewed as responsible for the giving of circumcision, yet the verse itself explicitly tells us that it was *not* Moses who gave it, but "the fathers." Thus to conclude that the emphasis of the perfect is to stress the responsibility of the subject, when in the same breath we are told that that is *not* the point, is surely an illegitimate outcome. There are other such problems with which McKay's version of stative aspect suffers.[4]

A different version of stative aspect is offered by Porter. Stative aspect, according to him, refers to a general state of affairs.[5] This conception's strength is that it removes focus from the subject of the verb, which is so problematic with stative conceptions of the perfect, and creates a general state.

> **John 12:23** ὁ δὲ Ἰησοῦς ἀποκρίνεται αὐτοῖς λέγων· **ἐλήλυθεν** ἡ ὥρα ἵνα δοξασθῇ ὁ υἱὸς τοῦ ἀνθρώπου.
>
> *And Jesus answered them, "The hour **has come** for the Son of Man to be glorified."*

According to Porter, the perfect in this verse indicates a new state of affairs: the hour has come, and now things are different. Porter's stative aspect seems to work well here, as indeed it does with many other examples.

There are, nevertheless, significant problems with this version of stative aspect too. To begin with, Porter's stative aspect is difficult to define and

---

3. McKay, *Syntax of the Verb*, 32.
4. See Campbell, *Indicative Mood*, 166–69.
5. Stanley E. Porter, *Idioms of the Greek New Testament* (2nd ed.; Biblical Languages: Greek 2; Sheffield: Sheffield Academic Press, 1994), 21–22.

does not parallel any kind of aspect in other languages. Furthermore, it is difficult to apply and sometimes results in quite forced exegesis, as the following example illustrates.

John 5:33 ὑμεῖς **ἀπεστάλκατε** πρὸς Ἰωάννην, καὶ **μεμαρτύρηκεν** τῇ ἀληθείᾳ.

*You sent to John, and **he has borne witness** to the truth.*

The question is: how do these two perfects indicate a new state of affairs? Are we to understand by the first perfect that there is a state of having-sent-to-John-ness? Does the second perfect refer to a state of John-having-witnessed-to-Jesus-ness? Again, there are several such difficulties with this version of stative aspect.[6]

Perhaps most serious of all, however, is the fact that stativity is not normally regarded as an aspectual value. Across all languages and in linguistic theory, stativity is an *Aktionsart* value, not an aspect.

Perfective Aspect

Fanning concludes as much about stative aspect—stativity is an *Aktionsart*, not an aspect.[7] His, and Olsen's, solution is to label the perfect tense-form as perfective in aspect, which at least works on the level of nomenclature. One of the reasons for regarding the perfect as perfective in aspect is because it is believed in academia that over the history of the Greek language the perfect eventually merged with the aorist in meaning.

Olsen regards the perfect as perfective in aspect and present in tense.[8] A fairly significant problem here is that there are many perfects that are not present referring, such as the ones in John 5:33 above. If present temporal reference is regarded as a semantic value of the perfect, many instances of usage of the perfect must go unaccounted.

Fanning, however, suggests a more complicated schema. He regards the perfect tense-form as perfective in aspect, present in temporal reference, and stative in *Aktionsart*.[9] In other words, Fanning posits three distinct semantic values: perfective aspect, present tense, and stative *Aktionsart*. Aside from the question of whether an *Aktionsart* value can

---

6. See Campbell, *Indicative Mood*, 169–75.

7. Buist M. Fanning, "Approaches to Verbal Aspect in New Testament Greek: Issues in Definition and Method," in *Biblical Greek Language and Linguistics: Open Questions in Current Research* (ed. Stanley E. Porter and D. A. Carson; JSNTS 80; Sheffield: Sheffield Academic Press, 1993), 49–50.

8. Olsen, *Aspect*, 202, 232.

be semantic, this conception raises other questions: what about perfects that are not stative? What about perfects that are not present in temporal reference?

A further problem with these models is that perfective aspect itself does not work well in explaining usage of the perfect tense-form. For example, perfective aspect does not accommodate stative lexemes well. Lexemes such as οἶδα are not accounted for under this model, and Fanning calls lexemes like this exceptions. It is worth noting that this means that approximately two-thirds of perfect usage in the New Testament is exceptional. On the contrary, this means that perfective aspect does not demonstrate enough power of explanation when it comes to the perfect tense-form.[10]

Imperfective Aspect

An overlooked fact in this debate is that the perfect parallels the present in its usage far more than it seems to do with the aorist. In fact, the patterns of perfect usage in narrative texts is virtually identical to those of the present. Nearly all perfect indicatives in narrative texts occur within discourse, just like the present. More than this, when the perfect does *not* occur within discourse, it demonstrates the same patterns as does the present when it is not within discourse. Just as the present forms historical presents with verbs of propulsion and introducers of discourse, so too does the perfect. Such evidence must provoke the question: does the perfect share the aspect of the present? Does the sharing of the same aspect account for these parallel patterns of usage?

I have argued extensively that the answer is "yes." Along with Evans, I argue that the perfect tense-form is imperfective in aspect, which is why it and the present tense-form behave so similarly.[11]

Not only does imperfective aspect explain the parallel usage of the perfect and present tense-forms, but it very nicely accommodates the many stative lexemes that are found in perfect usage. In most languages, imperfective aspect is the natural home of stativity. As such, this model of the perfect fits with what has always been observed — that the perfect often communicates stativity.

But imperfective aspect also is able to explain those perfects that are

---

9. Fanning, *Verbal Aspect*, 112–20.

10. See Campbell, *Indicative Mood*, 189–93.

11. See Campbell, *Indicative Mood*, 184–89; T. V. Evans, "Future Directions for Aspect Studies in Ancient Greek," in *Biblical Greek Language and Lexicography: Essays in Honor of Frederick W. Danker*, ed. Bernard A. Taylor et al. (Grand Rapids: Eerdmans, 2004), 206.

not stative; imperfective aspect can accommodate other types of lexemes too. It also explains past referring perfects that might seem to behave like aorists. Just as the present tense-form can be used to refer to the past (the historical present), so too can the perfect (the historical perfect). Consequently, imperfective aspect demonstrates the greatest power of explanation when it comes to the semantic meaning of the perfect tense-form.

Heightened Proximity

If, then, the perfect tense-form is imperfective in aspect, we must ask what it is that distinguishes it from the present and imperfect tense-forms. I argue that the perfect semantically encodes imperfective aspect and the spatial value of *heightened proximity*. In this way, the perfect is proximate like the present, but more so. This may be represented through the diagrams below.

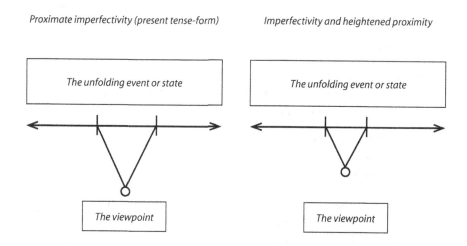

Proximate imperfectivity (present tense-form)   Imperfectivity and heightened proximity

The unfolding event or state   The unfolding event or state

The viewpoint   The viewpoint

Using again the illustration of the reporter and the street parade, the second diagram represents his taking a step closer to the parade. The parade is unfolding immediately before his eyes, as before, but now is even more proximate; he is viewing the action close up. The effect of this close-up view is that it concentrates the action by zooming in on it.

Heightened proximity, like proximity, is regarded as a semantic value alongside imperfective aspect. The perfect, therefore, semantically encodes imperfective aspect and the spatial value of heightened proximity. As such, it might be appropriate to think of the perfect as a *super-present*.

The Pluperfect Tense-Form

All agree that whatever aspect the perfect tense-form encodes, the pluperfect shares it. Typically the pluperfect is treated this way—as piggy-backing on the perfect—and therefore does not often receive due consideration on its own merit. By taking a close look at pluperfect usage, we discover that it is even harder to justify stative or perfective aspect than it is with the perfect. But it seems all the more clear that imperfective aspect has great power of explanation.

Just as the perfect parallels the usage of the present, so the pluperfect parallels the usage of the imperfect. It demonstrates the same functions within narrative, providing supplemental information that describes, explains, and gives background. This all fits well with imperfective aspect. It also fits well with the spatial value of remoteness. But if the pluperfect is distinct to the imperfect in its usage, it can function as providing information that is even more in the background than that provided by the imperfect. In other words, the pluperfect sometimes provides information that supplements information that is already supplemental, as the following example illustrates.

> **Mark 1:34** καὶ ἐθεράπευσεν πολλοὺς κακῶς ἔχοντας ποικίλαις νόσοις καὶ δαιμόνια πολλὰ ἐξέβαλεν καὶ οὐκ **ἤφιεν** λαλεῖν τὰ δαιμόνια, ὅτι **ᾔδεισαν** αὐτόν.
>
> *And he healed many who were sick with various diseases, and cast out many demons. And* **he would not permit** *the demons to speak, because* **they knew** *him.*

Here we see that the imperfect tense-form (bold and underlined) provides supplementary material; further description of the scene is given as we are told that Jesus did not permit the demons to speak. However, the pluperfect (bold) provides information that is supplemental to that supplemental information; we are told *why* Jesus did not allow the demons to speak—because they knew him.

Accordingly, the pluperfect is regarded as being more remote than the imperfect. Just as the perfect encodes heightened proximity in parallel to the proximity of the present, so the pluperfect encodes heightened remoteness in parallel to the remoteness of the imperfect. Thus, the pluperfect indicative semantically encodes imperfective aspect and the spatial value of heightened remoteness.

Part 2

Verbal Aspect and New Testament Text

Chapter 6

Verbal Lexeme Basics

—*෴*—

In order to examine the function of verbal aspect within New Testament text, we must first know something about verbal lexemes. The reason for this is that verbal aspect operates in cooperation with various lexemes to produce *Aktionsart* expression.

There are many different ways to analyze verbal lexemes. We will restrict our interest to the most important categorizations, which are directly relevant to our analysis of verbal pragmatics. Furthermore, our analysis would be strengthened by considering the range of usage of each lexeme by consulting a lexicon such as BDAG. We will at this stage, however, restrict our analysis to consideration of the gloss definition of each lexeme. With most lexemes, categorization is straightforward and unambiguous. There are, however, some lexemes for which categorization is a little ambiguous, but this should not give cause for concern.

The first decision we need to make when looking at a verbal lexeme is whether or not the lexeme is transitive or intransitive.

Transitive Lexemes

A lexeme is transitive if the action is *performed upon an object*. The action is performed by a subject and done *to* someone or something (the object). Whether or not a lexeme is transitive is decided simply by what the type of action is. In English, lexemes such as hit, give, kick, throw, arrange, and so on are all transitive. A person may hit *a target*, give *a gift*, kick *a ball*, throw *a javelin*, or arrange *a meeting*. We must note that, according to the definitions offered here, not all lexemes that take an object are necessarily transitive. The object must be *affected* or *impacted* somehow. So, for example, *to hear music* is not regarded here as transitive because the music is not affected by the action, even though it is the object of the action. To reiterate, for a lexeme to be transitive, there must be some kind of "exchange" from the subject to the object.[1]

Key question:
Is the action performed upon an object?
If yes = transitive lexeme

1. Transitive	2. Intransitive
performed upon an object	*not performed upon an object*

Intransitive Lexemes

If a lexeme is not transitive, it must be intransitive. An intransitive lexeme is one that does not require an object or does not perform an action upon its object. The action is performed by a subject, but it is not done *to* anyone or anything (though it may be done *with reference to* someone or something). In other words, an intransitive lexeme may take an object, but this must be *unaffected* by the action performed by the subject. For example, in the phrase *to hear music*, the hearer does not act on the music, even though it is the object of the verb. Whether or not a lexeme is intransitive is decided simply by what the type of action is. In English, lexemes such as sleep, know, live, die, and so on are all intransitive.

Key question:
Is the action performed upon an object?
If no = intransitive lexeme

Ambitransitive Lexemes

It is worth noting that some lexemes are difficult to categorize as either transitive or intransitive. The fact is that in most languages, there are certain lexemes that can be either transitive or intransitive, depending on the context. They may act upon an object in some situations (and so are

---

1. Linguists define transitivity in various ways, and this nuance is not always acknowledged. Lexemes are often labeled as transitive if they take an object at all. But we will adopt the more nuanced definition of transitivity, which requires the object to be affected.

transitive), or they may not act upon an object in other situations (and so are intransitive). These lexemes are best labelled "ambitransitive," because they can go either way. In English, lexemes such as eat, read, breathe, and so on are all ambitransitive. For example, *it's time to eat* is intransitive, but *I ate my lunch* is transitive. *He's breathing* is intransitive, but *we need to breath oxygen* is transitive.

Subcategories

Though it is possible to subcategorise transitive and intransitive verbs into several other types of lexemes, we will explore only two subcategories: punctiliar lexemes and stative lexemes.

Transitive: Punctiliar

If a lexeme is transitive, it may also be punctiliar. A punctiliar action is performed upon an object and is instantaneous in nature. It is a once-occurring, immediate type of action. Whether or not a lexeme is punctiliar is decided simply by what the type of action is. While a punctiliar action can be repeated, it cannot be drawn out for any length of time. In English, lexemes such as punch, kick, throw, and the like are all punctiliar. A person may punch a bag for two minutes, but this must be a series of punches; one punch cannot last for two minutes.

> **Key questions:**
>
> *Is the action performed upon an object?*
> *If yes = transitive*
>
> *Is the action instantaneous?*
> *If yes = punctiliar*

If a transitive lexeme is *not* punctiliar, we will simply call it transitive without specifying further. Examples of lexemes that are transitive but not punctiliar are give, arrange, defeat, and so on.

Intransitive: Stative

If a lexeme is intransitive, it may also be stative. A stative verb is not performed upon an object and describes a state of being. It is not time bound or progressive; it simply *is*. In fact, we may even consider a stative lexeme as a verb that is not really an *action*—it is simply a state. Whether or not a lexeme is stative is decided simply by what the type of action is. In English, lexemes such as know, trust, live, and so on are all stative.

Key questions:

Is the action performed upon an object?
If no = intransitive

Does the action describe a state of being?
If yes = stative

If an intransitive lexeme is *not* stative, we will simply call it intransitive without specifying further. Examples of lexemes that are intransitive but not stative are sleep, die, decide, and the like.

Transitive	Intransitive
performed upon an object	*not performed upon an object*
Punctiliar *instantaneous action*	**Stative** *state of being*

Some Greek Lexemes

Here are some common Greek verbs categorized into one of our four lexical categories. Note that some of these are not entirely clear but are affected by their lexical range of meaning and context. If a lexeme is capable of acting upon an object in some situations but does not act upon an object in others, it is categorized as ambitransitive. Since ambitransitive lexemes can behave like transitive lexemes or like intransitive lexemes, we should decide which way they are working in each context. Thus, for the sake of specific analysis in the following chapters, these lexemes will be described as either transitive or intransitive depending on whether or not they act upon an object in specific contexts (even though they are technically ambitransitive).

Lexeme	Gloss	Category
εἰμί	*to be*	intransitive: stative
ποιέω	*to do, make*	transitive
τίθημι	*to place, put*	transitive
βάλλω	*to throw*	transitive: punctiliar
εὑρίσκω	*to find*	transitive
ζητέω	*to seek*	transitive
φέρω	*to carry, bear*	transitive
ἔρχομαι	*to come, go*	intransitive
πορεύομαι	*to go*	intransitive
ἐγγίζω	*to draw near*	intransitive
λύω	*to loose, destroy*	transitive
ἐγείρω	*to raise up*	transitive
κάθημαι	*to be seated*	intransitive: stative
καθίζω	*to sit*	intransitive
λαμβάνω	*to take, receive*	transitive
τύπτω	*to strike*	transitive: punctiliar
ἅπτομαι	*to touch*	transitive: punctiliar
ἐσθίω	*to eat*	ambitransitive
καθεύδω	*to sleep*	intransitive
ζάω	*to live*	intransitive: stative
ὁράω	*to see*	ambitransitive
ἄγω	*to lead, go*	transitive/intransitive
ἀκολουθέω	*to follow*	intransitive
βλέπω	*to look at*	ambitransitive
ἀκούω	*to hear*	ambitransitive
θέλω	*to wish, desire*	intransitive: stative
βούλομαι	*to want*	intransitive: stative
ἀγαπάω	*to love*	ambitransitive
οἶδα	*to know*	intransitive: stative
γινώσκω	*to know*	intransitive: stative

Chapter 7

Present and Imperfect Tense-Forms

—◦◦◦◦—

Semantics

Verbal Aspect

The present and imperfect tense-forms encode imperfective aspect at the semantic level. Imperfective aspect views an action or state from the inside; it is the internal viewpoint. Using the illustration of the reporter and the street parade, the internal viewpoint is the view from the street, with the parade unfolding in full view. Unlike the view from afar (in the helicopter = perfective aspect), the reporter on the street does not view the beginning or end of the parade, but has a view of the details.

Spatial Qualities

Traditional approaches described the present and imperfect tense-forms as imperfective in aspect, with present and past tense respectively. Tense, however, is not here regarded as a semantic value; rather temporal reference is a pragmatic feature, determined in part by context. Instead, the present and imperfect tense-forms are regarded as semantically encoding the spatial values of proximity and remoteness respectively.

Thus, the present tense-form is imperfective in aspect, with the spatial value of proximity. The imperfect tense-form is imperfective in aspect, with the spatial value of remoteness. These are semantic values that are not cancelable but are expressed pragmatically in a variety of ways in context, which will be explored below.

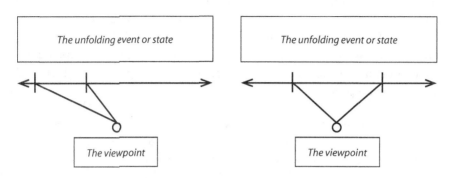

Remote imperfectivity (imperfect tense-form)   *Proximate imperfectivity (present tense-form)*

Pragmatics

Narrative Functions

Present Tense-Form

In narrative texts, the present indicative is most often found in discourse—direct discourse, indirect discourse, and authorial discourse, as illustrated by these examples.

John 5:20 ὁ γὰρ πατὴρ **φιλεῖ** τὸν υἱὸν καὶ πάντα **δείκνυσιν** αὐτῷ ἃ αὐτὸς **ποιεῖ**, καὶ μείζονα τούτων δείξει αὐτῷ ἔργα, ἵνα ὑμεῖς θαυμάζητε.

*For the Father **loves** the Son and **shows** him everything he **is doing**, and he will show him greater works than these so that you will be amazed.*

John 16:15 πάντα ὅσα **ἔχει** ὁ πατὴρ ἐμά ἐστιν· διὰ τοῦτο εἶπον ὅτι ἐκ τοῦ ἐμοῦ **λαμβάνει** καὶ ἀναγγελεῖ ὑμῖν.

*Everything the Father **has** is mine. This is why I told you that **he takes** from what is mine and will declare it to you.*

Discourse creates a proximate-imperfective context, as the speech or thought is presented immediately before the reader's eyes, as though unfolding. As such, the present indicative is attracted to discourse, being a proximate-imperfective tense-form. It is to be remembered, however, that the discourse function of the present tense-form is a pragmatic feature and is therefore cancelable.

Imperfect Tense-Form

The imperfect indicative, however, is most often found in narrative proper rather than discourse. Its normal function within narrative proper is to provide offline material. While aorists typically provide the skeletal structure of the narrative mainline, imperfects most often provide supplementary information that describes, characterizes, or explains, as illustrated by these examples.

John 5:18 διὰ τοῦτο οὖν μᾶλλον **ἐζήτουν** αὐτὸν οἱ Ἰουδαῖοι ἀποκτεῖναι, ὅτι οὐ μόνον **ἔλυεν** τὸ σάββατον, ἀλλὰ καὶ πατέρα ἴδιον **ἔλεγεν** τὸν θεὸν ἴσον ἑαυτὸν ποιῶν τῷ θεῷ.

*This is why the Jews **were seeking** all the more to kill him: not only **was he breaking** the Sabbath, but **he was** even **calling** God his own father, making himself equal with God.*

Luke 15:16 καὶ **ἐπεθύμει** χορτασθῆναι ἐκ τῶν κερατίων ὧν **ἤσθιον** οἱ χοῖροι, καὶ οὐδεὶς **ἐδίδου** αὐτῷ.

*He **was longing** to eat his fill from the carob pods the pigs **were eating**, but no one **would give** him any.*

Offline material is inherently remote-imperfective in nature, as the supplementary information provides an internal view (imperfective), but this is not presented as being immediately before the reader's eyes. It supplements the remote mainline and thus is remote in nature. As such, the imperfect indicative is attracted to offline material, since it is a remote-imperfective tense-form. It is to be remembered, however, that the offline function of the imperfect tense-form is a pragmatic feature and is therefore cancelable.

Aktionsart Interactions (Present Tense-Form)

Aktionsart refers to the way a verb behaves in the text when all features of the language and text bear upon it. There are three main elements that determine a particular verb's *Aktionsart*: semantics, lexeme, and context. There are, therefore, three steps required in order to ascertain what a verb is doing in the text:

1. Identify the semantic value of the verb.
2. Consider the lexeme and its interaction with the semantics.
3. Consider the context.

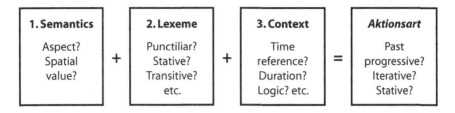

There are several ways in which the present tense-form functions pragmatically. Below are the most common and important *Aktionsart* descriptions of present usage and explanations of how the *Aktionsart* values are arrived at.

Progressive

Present tense-forms often end up depicting a process or action *in progress*. This is a common usage of the present tense-form and is a natural implicature of imperfective aspect. Imperfective aspect combines with any lexeme that is not punctiliar or stative to create a progressive sense. As long as this progressive sense is not overruled by context, the *Aktionsart* is progressive.

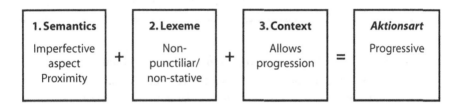

Luke 8:45 καὶ εἶπεν ὁ Ἰησοῦς· τίς ὁ ἁψάμενός μου; ἀρνουμένων δὲ πάντων εἶπεν ὁ Πέτρος· ἐπιστάτα, οἱ ὄχλοι **συνέχουσίν** σε καὶ **ἀποθλίβουσιν**.

*"Who touched me?" Jesus asked. When they all denied it, Peter said, "Master, the crowds **are hemming** you in and **pressing against** you."*

John 4:22 ὑμεῖς **προσκυνεῖτε** ὃ οὐκ οἴδατε· ἡμεῖς **προσκυνοῦμεν** ὃ οἴδαμεν, ὅτι ἡ σωτηρία ἐκ τῶν Ἰουδαίων ἐστίν.

*You [Samaritans] **worship** what you do not know. We **worship** what we do know, because salvation is from the Jews.*

Romans 8:17 εἰ δὲ τέκνα, καὶ κληρονόμοι· κληρονόμοι μὲν θεοῦ, συγκληρονόμοι δὲ Χριστοῦ, εἴπερ **συμπάσχομεν** ἵνα καὶ συνδοξασθῶμεν.

*... and if children, also heirs — heirs of God and coheirs with Christ — seeing that **we suffer** with him so that we may also be glorified with him.*

Stative

Present tense-forms often end up depicting a state. This is also a natural implicature of imperfective aspect. Imperfective aspect combines with a stative lexeme to create a stative *Aktionsart*, if this is not overturned by context. A stative lexeme is a word that describes a state of being rather than a process or transitive action. Sometimes the context can create a stative *Aktionsart* even if the lexeme is not in itself stative.

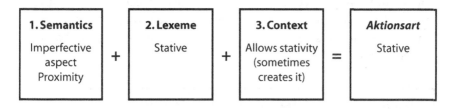

John 10:14–15 Ἐγώ εἰμι ὁ ποιμὴν ὁ καλὸς καὶ **γινώσκω** τὰ ἐμὰ καὶ **γινώσκουσί** με τὰ ἐμά, καθὼς **γινώσκει** με ὁ πατὴρ κἀγὼ **γινώσκω** τὸν πατέρα, καὶ τὴν ψυχήν μου τίθημι ὑπὲρ τῶν προβάτων.

*I am the good shepherd. I **know** my own sheep, and they **know** me, as the Father **knows** me, and I **know** the Father. I lay down my life for the sheep.*

Matthew 9:13 πορευθέντες δὲ μάθετε τί ἐστιν· ἔλεος **θέλω** καὶ οὐ θυσίαν· οὐ γὰρ ἦλθον καλέσαι δικαίους ἀλλὰ ἁμαρτωλούς.

*Go and learn what this means: **I desire** mercy and not sacrifice. For I didn't come to call the righteous, but sinners.*

Romans 6:8 εἰ δὲ ἀπεθάνομεν σὺν Χριστῷ, **πιστεύομεν** ὅτι καὶ συζήσομεν αὐτῷ.

*Now if we died with Christ, **we believe** that we will also live with Him.*

Iterative

Present tense-forms can depict iterative actions, which are events that repeatedly occur. There are two key ways in which an iterative *Aktionsart* may be created. First, imperfective aspect combines with a punctiliar lexeme, which creates the sense of a repeating punctiliar action. Second, imperfective aspect combines with any nonstative lexeme in a context that requires the action to be repeating.

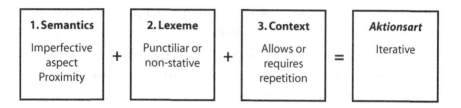

Matthew 17:15 καὶ λέγων· κύριε, ἐλέησόν μου τὸν υἱόν, ὅτι σεληνιάζεται καὶ κακῶς πάσχει· πολλάκις γὰρ **πίπτει** εἰς τὸ πῦρ καὶ πολλάκις εἰς τὸ ὕδωρ.

*"Lord," he said, "have mercy on my son, because he has seizures and suffers severely. He often **falls** into the fire and often into the water."*

Luke 9:39 καὶ ἰδοὺ πνεῦμα **λαμβάνει** αὐτὸν καὶ ἐξαίφνης **κράζει** καὶ **σπαράσσει** αὐτὸν μετὰ ἀφροῦ καὶ μόγις **ἀποχωρεῖ** ἀπ᾽ αὐτοῦ συντρῖβον αὐτόν.

*Often a spirit **seizes** him; suddenly **he shrieks**, and it **throws** him **into convulsions** until he foams at the mouth; wounding him, it hardly ever **leaves** him.*

Luke 18:12 **νηστεύω** δὶς τοῦ σαββάτου, **ἀποδεκατῶ** πάντα ὅσα κτῶμαι.

*I **fast** twice a week; I **give a tenth** of everything I get.*

Gnomic

Present tense-forms can depict gnomic actions, which are universal and timeless. A gnomic *Aktionsart* is created through the combination of imperfective aspect and a context in which generic statements are made. These may involve any type of lexeme.

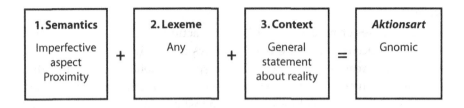

Matthew 5:32 ἐγὼ δὲ λέγω ὑμῖν ὅτι πᾶς ὁ ἀπολύων τὴν γυναῖκα αὐτοῦ παρεκτὸς λόγου πορνείας **ποιεῖ** αὐτὴν μοιχευθῆναι, καὶ ὃς ἐὰν ἀπολελυμένην γαμήσῃ, **μοιχᾶται**.

*But I tell you, everyone who divorces his wife, except in a case of sexual immorality, **causes** her to commit adultery. And whoever marries a divorced woman **commits adultery**.*

John 3:8 τὸ πνεῦμα ὅπου **θέλει πνεῖ** καὶ τὴν φωνὴν αὐτοῦ **ἀκούεις**, ἀλλ᾽ οὐκ οἶδας πόθεν **ἔρχεται** καὶ ποῦ **ὑπάγει**· οὕτως **ἐστὶν** πᾶς ὁ γεγεννημένος ἐκ τοῦ πνεύματος.

*The wind **blows** where **it pleases**, and **you hear** its sound, but you don't know where **it comes** from or where **it is going**. So **it is** with everyone born of the Spirit.*

John 5:24 Ἀμὴν ἀμὴν λέγω ὑμῖν ὅτι ὁ τὸν λόγον μου ἀκούων καὶ πιστεύων τῷ πέμψαντί με **ἔχει** ζωὴν αἰώνιον καὶ εἰς κρίσιν **οὐκ ἔρχεται**, ἀλλὰ μεταβέβηκεν ἐκ τοῦ θανάτου εἰς τὴν ζωήν.

*I assure you: Anyone who hears my word and believes him who sent me **has** eternal life and **will not come** under judgment but has passed from death to life.*

Historical Present

The present tense-form is often used in nonpresent contexts, most often past-referring. These are best translated like aorists, though they are not the same as aorists in meaning. There are two basic types of historical presents: those that introduce discourse and those that employ lexemes of propulsion.

First, the historical presents that introduce discourse utilize the present tense-form because they are leading into a proximate-imperfective context (discourse). In such cases, the proximate-imperfective nature of discourse "spills over" to the verb that introduces it.

Second, lexemes of propulsion are verbs that convey transition—the movement from one point to another. These include verbs of coming and going, lifting, taking, giving, and so on. The proximate-imperfective nature of the present tense-form combines with these lexemes in order to highlight the transition that is conveyed. There is no obvious way to convey this in translation.

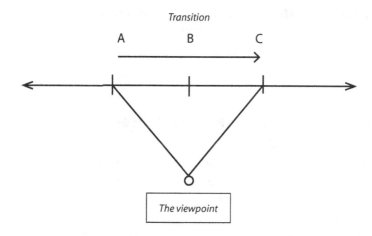

Proximate imperfectivity and heightened transition

This diagram demonstrates that an imperfective-proximate depiction of an action may heighten the sense of transition as the action moves from point A to C. The transition is heightened because, in moving from A to C, point B is crossed, which is the author/speaker's center of reference in his or her imperfective viewpoint. The author/speaker, in a sense, views the action as passing in front of him or her and moving from one side of point B to the other side of point B. This movement from A, past B, to C is the element that heightens the transition in verbs of propulsion.

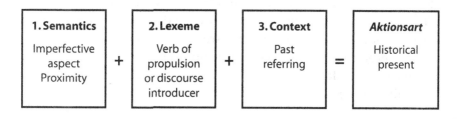

Mark 3:20 Καὶ **ἔρχεται** εἰς οἶκον· καὶ **συνέρχεται** πάλιν [ὁ] ὄχλος, ὥστε μὴ δύνασθαι αὐτοὺς μηδὲ ἄρτον φαγεῖν.

*Then **he went** home, and the crowd **gathered** again so that they were not even able to eat.*

Mark 5:22 Καὶ **ἔρχεται** εἷς τῶν ἀρχισυναγώγων, ὀνόματι Ἰάϊρος, καὶ ἰδὼν αὐτὸν **πίπτει** πρὸς τοὺς πόδας αὐτοῦ.

*One of the synagogue leaders, named Jairus, **came**, and when he saw Jesus, **he fell** at his feet.*

John 19:28 Μετὰ τοῦτο εἰδὼς ὁ Ἰησοῦς ὅτι ἤδη πάντα τετέλεσται, ἵνα τελειωθῇ ἡ γραφή, **λέγει**· διψῶ.

*After this, when Jesus knew that everything was now accomplished that the Scripture might be fulfilled, **he said**, "I'm thirsty!"*

Nonindicative Usage (Present Tense-Form)
Subjunctive Mood
Students of Greek often have difficulty working out what meaningful difference there is between aorist and present subjunctives. This is especially the case when we are taught to translate both as *I might loose,* or some variation of this gloss. If both subjunctives translate this way, why did Greek authors choose one over the other? Why does the language need more than one tense-form in the subjunctive mood?

The simplest answer is that sometimes languages make distinctions that other languages do not. Just because we might translate a present and an aorist subjunctive the same way in English does not mean that there was no distinguishable difference to the Greek speaker. It might simply mean that we have no real way of communicating the difference. But that does not mean that the student of Greek should not appreciate the original distinction.

Another reason for our difficulty in handling subjunctives may have to do with the fact that the *only* difference between them is verbal aspect. Regardless of one's position on the question of tense in the indicative mood, all agree that nonindicatives are aspectual and do not encode temporal reference at the semantic level. Some students, however, will struggle to conceive of actions that don't have any temporal reference at all, even at the pragmatic level. How may an action in the subjunctive mood be viewed internally? How may it be viewed externally?

It may help to approach the distinction through pragmatic features. As with aspect in the indicative mood, aspect in the subjunctive mood issues a range of pragmatic implicatures, which typically arise from one aspect or the other. Just as there is a predictable range of pragmatic expressions that arise from imperfective aspect in the indicative mood, so too is there a predictable range of expressions that arise from imperfective aspect in the subjunctive mood. Getting a handle on these will help to grasp the differences that aspect makes in this mood.

While it may be difficult to discern for English speakers, verbal aspect is fully operational within the Greek subjunctive mood. The use of the present subjunctive reveals regular expressions of imperfective aspect, viewing the action internally. Some common implicatures of imperfective aspect within present subjunctives are activities that are conceptually unfolding, temporally ongoing, stative, or personally characteristic.[1] These examples demonstrate the internal viewpoint of the imperfective aspect conveyed by the present subjunctive.

Luke 5:12 Καὶ ἐγένετο ἐν τῷ εἶναι αὐτὸν ἐν μιᾷ τῶν πόλεων καὶ ἰδοὺ ἀνὴρ πλήρης λέπρας· ἰδὼν δὲ τὸν Ἰησοῦν, πεσὼν ἐπὶ πρόσωπον ἐδεήθη αὐτοῦ λέγων· κύριε, ἐὰν **θέλῃς** δύνασαί με καθαρίσαι.

*When he was in one of the cities, there was a man full of leprosy. And when he saw Jesus, he fell on his face and begged him, "Lord, if **you are willing**, you can make me clean."*

John 15:2 πᾶν κλῆμα ἐν ἐμοὶ μὴ φέρον καρπὸν αἴρει αὐτό, καὶ πᾶν τὸ καρπὸν φέρον καθαίρει αὐτὸ ἵνα καρπὸν πλείονα **φέρῃ**.

*Every branch in me that does not bear fruit he takes away, and every branch that does bear fruit he prunes, that **it may bear** more fruit.*

In these instances, the imperfective aspect of the present subjunctives allow a stative implicature: *to be willing* and *to bear fruit* describe certain characteristics of their grammatical subjects; the tree has fruit on it. Stativity is one of the natural expressions of imperfective aspect.

Furthermore, its imperfective aspect makes the present subjunctive especially suited to proverbial, general, and generic statements, as seen below. This is a key pragmatic function of imperfective aspect within the subjunctive mood.

---

1. Campbell, *Non-Indicatives*, 54.

John 17:3 αὕτη δέ ἐστιν ἡ αἰώνιος ζωὴ ἵνα **γινώσκωσιν** σὲ τὸν μόνον ἀληθινὸν θεὸν καὶ ὃν ἀπέστειλας Ἰησοῦν Χριστόν.

*This is eternal life, that **they might know** you, the only true God, and the one you have sent — Jesus Christ.*

Luke 11:33 Οὐδεὶς λύχνον ἅψας εἰς κρύπτην τίθησιν [οὐδὲ ὑπὸ τὸν μόδιον] ἀλλ᾽ ἐπὶ τὴν λυχνίαν, ἵνα οἱ εἰσπορευόμενοι τὸ φῶς **βλέπωσιν**.

*No one after lighting a lamp puts it in a cellar or under a basket, but on a lampstand, so that those who come in **may see** the light.*

Imperative Mood

The present imperative semantically encodes imperfective aspect. Within present imperatival usage, imperfective aspect normally implicates commands that express some kind of general instruction.[2] This is due to the fact that imperfective aspect is open-ended, without the beginning or end of the action in view. Such a view is inherently suited to the portrayal of instructions that are general in intent. A general instruction is one that is issued with reference to a general situation, or perhaps more accurately, situations in general. Accordingly, it is often employed for the issuing of ethical and moral instruction that is to be characteristic of its adherents. It must be stressed, however, that this is a pragmatic function of imperfective aspect in the imperative mood and as such is cancelable.

To suggest that the present imperative conveys general instruction does not imply that the intended action is to be *continuous* in nature. Such a conclusion confuses aspect with *Aktionsart* in a similar manner to the mistake of concluding that the present indicative must always implicate continuous action, which it does not. Thus the present imperative issues a general command, but not necessarily a *continuous* command. The examples below demonstrate general instructions issued with the present imperative.

---

2. The distinction between general commands (issued by the present imperative) and specific commands (issued by the aorist imperative) is controversial, and Fanning and Porter reach opposite conclusions about it. While Fanning affirms the distinction, Porter rejects it, and yet it is possible to mediate the two positions. In short, if the general/specific command distinction is held as semantic, it must fail, for there are numerous "exceptions." However, if the distinction is regarded as pragmatic, Porter's objections may be mollified. See Campbell, *Non-Indicative Verbs*, 81–83.

Luke 6:27 Ἀλλὰ ὑμῖν λέγω τοῖς ἀκούουσιν· **ἀγαπᾶτε** τοὺς ἐχθροὺς ὑμῶν, καλῶς **ποιεῖτε** τοῖς μισοῦσιν ὑμᾶς.

*But I say to you who hear, **love** your enemies, **do** good to those who hate you.*

Luke 14:35 οὔτε εἰς γῆν οὔτε εἰς κοπρίαν εὔθετόν ἐστιν, ἔξω βάλλουσιν αὐτό. ὁ ἔχων ὦτα ἀκούειν **ἀκουέτω**.

*It is fit neither for the land nor for the manure pile; it is thrown away. He who has ears to hear, **let him hear**.*

John 21:16 λέγει αὐτῷ πάλιν δεύτερον· Σίμων Ἰωάννου, ἀγαπᾷς με; λέγει αὐτῷ· ναὶ κύριε, σὺ οἶδας ὅτι φιλῶ σε. λέγει αὐτῷ· **ποίμαινε** τὰ πρόβατά μου.

*He said to him a second time, "Simon, son of John, do you love me?" He said to him, "Yes, Lord; you know that I love you." He said to him, "**Shepherd** my sheep."*

Certain lexemes used with the present imperative, however, express specific commands instead of general commands. Interestingly, these verbs are of the same lexical type that typically form historical presents when in the indicative mood: verbs of propulsion and verbs of speaking. Note these examples:

John 14:31 ἀλλ' ἵνα γνῷ ὁ κόσμος ὅτι ἀγαπῶ τὸν πατέρα, καὶ καθὼς ἐνετείλατό μοι ὁ πατήρ, οὕτως ποιῶ. **ἐγείρεσθε**, ἄγωμεν ἐντεῦθεν.

*But that the world may know that I love the Father, I do as the Father has commanded me. **Rise**, let us go from here.*

John 2:8 καὶ λέγει αὐτοῖς· ἀντλήσατε νῦν καὶ **φέρετε** τῷ ἀρχιτρικλίνῳ· οἱ δὲ ἤνεγκαν.

*And he said to them, "Now draw some out and **take** it to the master of the banquet." So they took it.*

Acts 22:27 προσελθὼν δὲ ὁ χιλίαρχος εἶπεν αὐτῷ· **λέγε** μοι, σὺ Ῥωμαῖος εἶ; ὁ δὲ ἔφη· ναί.

*The commander came and said to him, "**Tell** me, are you a Roman citizen?" And he said, "Yes."*

These examples demonstrate that with verbs of propulsion and speaking, the present imperative takes on a usage that would normally be associated with the aorist imperative; the actions are specific rather than general. As with the historical present in the indicative mood, the present imperative may be used with verbs of propulsion to highlight the transition inherent to such lexemes.

Participle

The present participle semantically encodes imperfective aspect. It is its aspect that leads to the present participle's main pragmatic function in that it nearly always expresses action that is contemporaneous with its leading verb (excluding substantival and periphrastic usages).

John 6:24 ὅτε οὖν εἶδεν ὁ ὄχλος ὅτι Ἰησοῦς οὐκ ἔστιν ἐκεῖ οὐδὲ οἱ μαθηταὶ αὐτοῦ, ἐνέβησαν αὐτοὶ εἰς τὰ πλοιάρια καὶ ἦλθον εἰς Καφαρναοὺμ **ζητοῦντες** τὸν Ἰησοῦν.

*So when the crowd saw that Jesus was not there, nor his disciples, they got into the boats and went to Capernaum, **seeking** Jesus.*

While the present participle may at times depict an action that has begun before the action of the leading verb has begun, it is not viewed as completed before the second action begins, but rather remains "open."

Acts 9:33 εὗρεν δὲ ἐκεῖ ἄνθρωπόν τινα ὀνόματι Αἰνέαν ἐξ ἐτῶν ὀκτὼ **κατακείμενον** ἐπὶ κραβάττου, ὃς ἦν παραλελυμένος.

*There he found a man named Aeneas, who was paralyzed and had been **bedridden** for eight years.*

Thus this present participle depicts a situation that, while antecedent in origin, becomes contemporaneous with the action of the leading verb. The present participle will not normally be found depicting an action that is completed before the action of the leading verb begins.

Infinitive

Though difficult to appreciate at times, present infinitives semantically encode imperfective aspect. This aspect is pragmatically expressed in a variety of ways, with the primary function to be found within particular infinitival constructions: the usage of the present infinitive is mostly determined through infinitival constructions that commonly require it.

For many of these constructions, the preference for the present infinitive is clearly due to its imperfective aspect.

Two key constructions are of the type *"begin to ..."* and *"about to ..."* — as illustrated by the examples below. To portray an action as *beginning* is to choose an unfolding view of the action; an internal view gives attention to an action's unfolding and thus is able to accommodate the portrayal of the beginning of the action. Similarly, to portray an action as *about to* begin or take place is simply the latter concept removed by one step; the beginning of the action is imminent and is almost in view.

Luke 5:21 καὶ **ἤρξαντο διαλογίζεσθαι** οἱ γραμματεῖς καὶ οἱ Φαρισαῖοι λέγοντες· τίς ἐστιν οὗτος ὃς λαλεῖ βλασφημίας; τίς δύναται ἁμαρτίας ἀφεῖναι εἰ μὴ μόνος ὁ θεός;

*Then the scribes and the Pharisees **began to question**, saying, "Who is this, who speaks blasphemies? Who can forgive sins but God alone?"*

Luke 15:14 δαπανήσαντος δὲ αὐτοῦ πάντα ἐγένετο λιμὸς ἰσχυρὰ κατὰ τὴν χώραν ἐκείνην, καὶ αὐτὸς **ἤρξατο ὑστερεῖσθαι.**

*After he had spent everything, a severe famine struck that country, and **he began to be in need**.*

John 4:47 οὗτος ἀκούσας ὅτι Ἰησοῦς ἥκει ἐκ τῆς Ἰουδαίας εἰς τὴν Γαλιλαίαν ἀπῆλθεν πρὸς αὐτὸν καὶ ἠρώτα ἵνα καταβῇ καὶ ἰάσηται αὐτοῦ τὸν υἱόν, **ἤμελλεν** γὰρ **ἀποθνῄσκειν.**

*When he heard that Jesus had come from Judea to Galilee, he went to him and asked him to come down and heal his son, for **he was about to die**.*

Another construction that is commonly used with the present infinitive is ἐν τῷ + *infinitive* for contemporaneous time. This expresses an action that occurs while something else in the narrative takes place. Most often the construction expresses an open-ended action that is intersected by some other action. Since imperfective aspect portrays actions internally and as though unfolding, its suitability both to contemporaneous time and open-ended action should be obvious.

Mark 4:4 καὶ ἐγένετο **ἐν τῷ σπείρειν** ὃ μὲν ἔπεσεν παρὰ τὴν ὁδόν, καὶ ἦλθεν τὰ πετεινὰ καὶ κατέφαγεν αὐτό.

*As **he sowed**, some seed fell along the path, and the birds came and ate it up.*

Luke 9:29 καὶ ἐγένετο **ἐν τῷ προσεύχεσθαι** αὐτὸν τὸ εἶδος τοῦ προσώπου αὐτοῦ ἕτερον καὶ ὁ ἱματισμὸς αὐτοῦ λευκὸς ἐξαστράπτων.

*And **while he was praying**, the appearance of his face changed, and his clothes became dazzling white.*

Luke 17:14 καὶ ἰδὼν εἶπεν αὐτοῖς· πορευθέντες ἐπιδείξατε ἑαυτοὺς τοῖς ἱερεῦσιν. καὶ ἐγένετο **ἐν τῷ ὑπάγειν** αὐτοὺς ἐκαθαρίσθησαν.

*When he saw them he said to them, "Go and show yourselves to the priests." And **as they went** they were cleansed.*

Yet another construction that is nearly always used with the present infinitive is the causal **διὰ τὸ** + *infinitive* construction. The causal infinitive explains the reasons behind various mainline actions, and thus this construction is unsurprisingly dominated by the present infinitive due to its imperfective aspect, in the same way that offline information is conveyed through imperfective aspect in the indicative mood.

Luke 8:6 καὶ ἕτερον κατέπεσεν ἐπὶ τὴν πέτραν, καὶ φυὲν ἐξηράνθη **διὰ τὸ μὴ ἔχειν** ἰκμάδα.

*Some fell on the rock, and when it grew up, it withered away, **because it had no** moisture.*

Luke 18:5 **διά γε τὸ παρέχειν** μοι κόπον τὴν χήραν ταύτην ἐκδικήσω αὐτήν, ἵνα μὴ εἰς τέλος ἐρχομένη ὑπωπιάζῃ με.

*" ... yet **because** this widow **troubles** me, I will give her justice, so that she doesn't wear me out by her coming."*

John 2:24 αὐτὸς δὲ Ἰησοῦς οὐκ ἐπίστευεν αὐτὸν αὐτοῖς **διὰ τὸ** αὐτὸν **γινώσκειν** πάντας.

*But Jesus did not entrust himself to them, **because** he **knew** all people.*

Such infinitival constructions account for the majority of present infinitival usage. As for those that do not function within these constructions, the unifying characteristics of present infinitives are related to the portrayal of events, actions, or descriptions in a manner that is simply best described as internal in viewpoint.

Aktionsart Interactions (Imperfect Tense-Form)

There are several ways in which the imperfect tense-form functions pragmatically. Below are the most common and important *Aktionsart* descriptions of imperfect usage and explanations of how the *Aktionsart* values are arrived at.

Progressive

Imperfect tense-forms often end up depicting a process or action *in progress*. This is a common usage of the imperfect tense-form and is a natural implicature of imperfective aspect. Imperfective aspect combines with any lexeme that is not punctiliar or stative to create a progressive sense. As long as this progressive sense is not overruled by context, the *Aktionsart* is progressive.

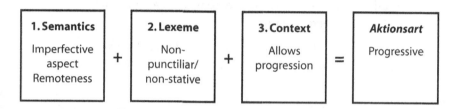

Matthew 14:36 καὶ **παρεκάλουν** αὐτὸν ἵνα μόνον ἅψωνται τοῦ κρασπέδου τοῦ ἱματίου αὐτοῦ· καὶ ὅσοι ἥψαντο διεσώθησαν.

They were begging him that they might only touch the tassel on his robe. And as many as touched it were made perfectly well.

Mark 5:24 καὶ ἀπῆλθεν μετ᾽ αὐτοῦ. καὶ **ἠκολούθει** αὐτῷ ὄχλος πολὺς καὶ **συνέθλιβον** αὐτόν.

So Jesus went with him, and a large crowd was following and pressing against him.

John 7:25 Ἔλεγον οὖν τινες ἐκ τῶν Ἱεροσολυμιτῶν· οὐχ οὗτός ἐστιν ὃν ζητοῦσιν ἀποκτεῖναι;

Some of the people of Jerusalem were saying, "Isn't this the man they want to kill?"

Stative

Imperfect tense-forms often end up depicting a state. This is also a natural implicature of imperfective aspect. Imperfective aspect combines with a stative lexeme to create a stative *Aktionsart*, if this is not overturned by context. A stative lexeme is a word that describes a state of being rather than a process or transitive action. Sometimes the context can create a stative *Aktionsart* even if the lexeme is not in itself stative.

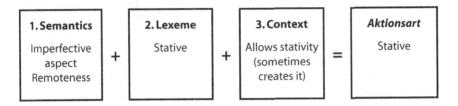

Mark 1:16 Καὶ παράγων παρὰ τὴν θάλασσαν τῆς Γαλιλαίας εἶδεν Σίμωνα καὶ Ἀνδρέαν τὸν ἀδελφὸν Σίμωνος ἀμφιβάλλοντας ἐν τῇ θαλάσσῃ· **ἦσαν** γὰρ ἁλιεῖς.

*As he was passing along by the Sea of Galilee, he saw Simon and Andrew, Simon's brother. They were casting a net into the sea, since **they were** fishermen.*

John 2:25 καὶ ὅτι οὐ χρείαν **εἶχεν** ἵνα τις μαρτυρήσῃ περὶ τοῦ ἀνθρώπου· αὐτὸς γὰρ **ἐγίνωσκεν** τί ἦν ἐν τῷ ἀνθρώπῳ.

*... and because he did not **need** anyone to testify about man; for he himself **knew** what was in man.*

John 6:21 **ἤθελον** οὖν λαβεῖν αὐτὸν εἰς τὸ πλοῖον, καὶ εὐθέως ἐγένετο τὸ πλοῖον ἐπὶ τῆς γῆς εἰς ἣν ὑπῆγον.

*Then **they were willing** to take him on board, and at once the boat was at the shore where they were heading.*

Ingressive

The imperfect tense-form is able to depict the beginning, and subsequent progression, of an action. This is similar to the progressive *Aktionsart*, but differs in that the beginning of the action is in view. Most often the beginning of an action is flagged by the context, in which there is some kind of shift or new direction in the narrative.

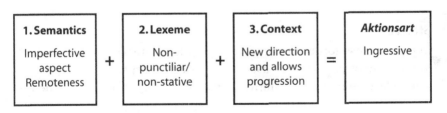

Matthew 5:2 καὶ ἀνοίξας τὸ στόμα αὐτοῦ **ἐδίδασκεν** αὐτοὺς λέγων·

*Then **he began to teach** them, saying…*

Luke 4:39 καὶ ἐπιστὰς ἐπάνω αὐτῆς ἐπετίμησεν τῷ πυρετῷ καὶ ἀφῆκεν αὐτήν· παραχρῆμα δὲ ἀναστᾶσα **διηκόνει** αὐτοῖς.

*So he stood over her and rebuked the fever, and it left her. She got up immediately and **began to serve** them.*

John 5:16 καὶ διὰ τοῦτο **ἐδίωκον** οἱ Ἰουδαῖοι τὸν Ἰησοῦν, ὅτι ταῦτα ἐποίει ἐν σαββάτῳ.

*Therefore, the Jews **began persecuting** Jesus because he was doing these things on the Sabbath.*

Iterative

Imperfect tense-forms can depict iterative actions, which are events that repeatedly occur. There are two key ways in which an iterative *Aktionsart* may be created. First, imperfective aspect combines with a punctiliar lexeme, which creates the sense of a repeating punctiliar action. Second, imperfective aspect combines with any nonstative lexeme in a context that requires the action to be repetition.

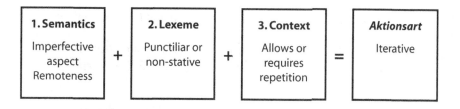

Matthew 26:55 Ἐν ἐκείνῃ τῇ ὥρᾳ εἶπεν ὁ Ἰησοῦς τοῖς ὄχλοις· ὡς ἐπὶ λῃστὴν ἐξήλθατε μετὰ μαχαιρῶν καὶ ξύλων συλλαβεῖν με; καθ᾽ ἡμέραν ἐν τῷ ἱερῷ **ἐκαθεζόμην** διδάσκων καὶ οὐκ ἐκρατήσατέ με.

*At that time Jesus said to the crowds, "Have you come out with swords and clubs, as if I were a criminal, to capture me? Every day **I used to sit**, teaching in the temple complex, and you didn't arrest me."*

Matthew 27:30 καὶ ἐμπτύσαντες εἰς αὐτὸν ἔλαβον τὸν κάλαμον καὶ **ἔτυπτον** εἰς τὴν κεφαλὴν αὐτοῦ.

*Then they spit at him, took the reed, and **kept hitting** him on the head.*

John 3:22 Μετὰ ταῦτα ἦλθεν ὁ Ἰησοῦς καὶ οἱ μαθηταὶ αὐτοῦ εἰς τὴν Ἰουδαίαν γῆν καὶ ἐκεῖ διέτριβεν μετ᾽ αὐτῶν καὶ **ἐβάπτιζεν**.

*After this, Jesus and his disciples went to the Judean countryside, where he spent time with them and **was baptizing**.*

Conative

The imperfect tense-form is sometimes used to portray an action that is attempted but not accomplished. In such cases, the imperfective aspect combines with any nonstative lexical type to present an action as being undertaken but not completed. It will always be the context that demands a conative *Aktionsart*. When the context makes it clear that the action was attempted but not achieved, a conative reading ensues.

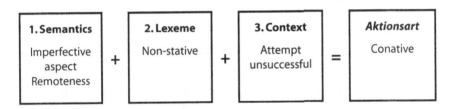

Mark 15:23 καὶ **ἐδίδουν** αὐτῷ ἐσμυρνισμένον οἶνον· ὃς δὲ οὐκ ἔλαβεν.

*They **tried to give** him wine mixed with myrrh, but he did not take it.*

Luke 1:59 Καὶ ἐγένετο ἐν τῇ ἡμέρᾳ τῇ ὀγδόῃ ἦλθον περιτεμεῖν τὸ παιδίον καὶ **ἐκάλουν** αὐτὸ ἐπὶ τῷ ὀνόματι τοῦ πατρὸς αὐτοῦ Ζαχαρίαν.

*When they came to circumcise the child on the eighth day, **they were going to call** him by the name Zechariah, after his father.*

Acts 7:26 τῇ τε ἐπιούσῃ ἡμέρᾳ ὤφθη αὐτοῖς μαχομένοις καὶ **συνήλλασσεν** αὐτοὺς εἰς εἰρήνην εἰπών· ἄνδρες, ἀδελφοί ἐστε· ἱνατί ἀδικεῖτε ἀλλήλους;

*The next day he showed up while they were fighting and **tried to reconcile** them peacefully, saying, "Men, you are brothers. Why are you mistreating each other?"*

Exercises for Present and Imperfect Tense-Forms

For each passage, (1) write about the semantic meaning of the verb, (2) state the contribution of the lexeme, and (3) discuss the function of the verb in context. Once you have written your answers, summarize your findings in the boxes below each passage.

Example:

Luke 8:45 (x2) καὶ εἶπεν ὁ Ἰησοῦς· τίς ὁ ἁψάμενός μου; ἀρνουμένων δὲ πάντων εἶπεν ὁ Πέτρος· ἐπιστάτα, οἱ ὄχλοι **συνέχουσίν** σε καὶ **ἀποθλίβουσιν.**

*"Who touched me?" Jesus asked. When they all denied it, Peter said, "Master, the crowds **are hemming** you **in** and **pressing against you.**"*

1. Semantic meaning of the verb. The present indicative semantically encodes imperfective aspect and the spatial value of proximity.

2. Contribution of the lexeme. The lexemes are transitive (perform an action upon an object). They are not punctiliar or stative.

3. Function in context. The context makes it clear that these actions are taking place continuously at the time of speech. Thus, these verbs are conveying progressive action.

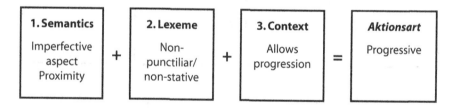

John 7:42 οὐχ ἡ γραφὴ εἶπεν ὅτι ἐκ τοῦ σπέρματος Δαυὶδ καὶ ἀπὸ Βηθλέεμ τῆς κώμης ὅπου ἦν Δαυὶδ **ἔρχεται** ὁ χριστός;

*"Doesn't the Scripture say that the Christ **comes** from David's offspring and from the town of Bethlehem, where David once lived?"*

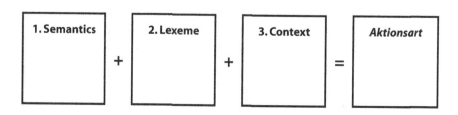

John 5:16 καὶ διὰ τοῦτο **ἐδίωκον** οἱ Ἰουδαῖοι τὸν Ἰησοῦν, ὅτι ταῦτα ἐποίει ἐν σαββάτῳ.

*Therefore, the Jews **began persecuting** Jesus because he was doing these things on the Sabbath.*

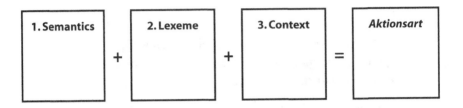

Romans 1:18 Ἀποκαλύπτεται γὰρ ὀργὴ θεοῦ ἀπ᾽ οὐρανοῦ ἐπὶ πᾶσαν ἀσέβειαν καὶ ἀδικίαν ἀνθρώπων τῶν τὴν ἀλήθειαν ἐν ἀδικίᾳ κατεχόντων.

*For God's wrath **is revealed** from heaven against all godlessness and unrighteousness of people who by their unrighteousness suppress the truth.*

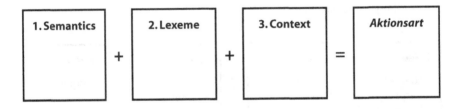

Romans 8:3 Τὸ γὰρ ἀδύνατον τοῦ νόμου ἐν ᾧ **ἠσθένει** διὰ τῆς σαρκός, ὁ θεὸς τὸν ἑαυτοῦ υἱὸν πέμψας ἐν ὁμοιώματι σαρκὸς ἁμαρτίας καὶ περὶ ἁμαρτίας κατέκρινεν τὴν ἁμαρτίαν ἐν τῇ σαρκί.

*What the law could not do since **it was limited** by the flesh, God did. He condemned sin in the flesh by sending his own Son in flesh like ours under sin's domain, and as a sin offering.*

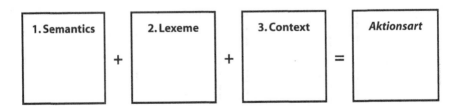

John 15:27 (x2) καὶ ὑμεῖς δὲ **μαρτυρεῖτε**, ὅτι ἀπ' ἀρχῆς μετ' ἐμοῦ **ἐστε**.

*You also **will testify**, because you **have been** with me from the beginning.*

1. Semantics		2. Lexeme		3. Context		Aktionsart
	+		+		=	

Romans 6:8 εἰ δὲ ἀπεθάνομεν σὺν Χριστῷ, **πιστεύομεν** ὅτι καὶ συζήσομεν αὐτῷ.

*Now if we died with Christ, **we believe** that we will also live with him.*

1. Semantics		2. Lexeme		3. Context		Aktionsart
	+		+		=	

John 3:22 Μετὰ ταῦτα ἦλθεν ὁ Ἰησοῦς καὶ οἱ μαθηταὶ αὐτοῦ εἰς τὴν Ἰουδαίαν γῆν καὶ ἐκεῖ διέτριβεν μετ' αὐτῶν καὶ **ἐβάπτιζεν**.

*After this, Jesus and his disciples went to the Judean countryside, where he spent time with them and **was baptizing**.*

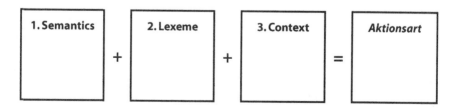

Romans 8:13 (x3) εἰ γὰρ κατὰ σάρκα **ζῆτε**, **μέλλετε** ἀποθνῄσκειν· εἰ δὲ πνεύματι τὰς πράξεις τοῦ σώματος **θανατοῦτε**, ζήσεσθε.

*… for if **you live** according to the flesh, **you are going** to die. But if by the Spirit **you put to death** the deeds of the body, you will live.*

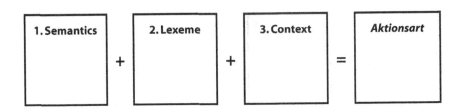

Chapter 8

Aorist and Future Tense-Forms

—◈—

Semantics

Verbal Aspect

The aorist tense-form encodes perfective aspect at the semantic level. Perfective aspect views an action or state from the outside; it is the external viewpoint. Using the illustration of the reporter and the street parade, the external viewpoint is the view from the helicopter, with the parade seen as a whole. Unlike the close-up view (from the street = imperfective aspect), the reporter in the helicopter does not view the parade's details or how it unfolds, but has an external view of the whole event.

The verbal aspect of the future tense-form is a matter of debate, with options ranging from nonaspectual, perfective, imperfective, or both perfective and imperfective. In part, this confusion stems from the difficult nature of *futurity* when applied to understanding verbal meaning and function. Nevertheless, regarding the future as encoding perfective aspect provides the best power of explanation, and therefore that is the position adopted here.[1]

Spatial/Temporal Qualities

Traditional approaches described the aorist tense-form as perfective in aspect, with past tense. Tense, however, is not here regarded as a semantic value; rather, temporal reference is a pragmatic feature, determined in part by context. Instead, the aorist tense-form is regarded as semantically

---

1. For extensive argumentation along such lines, see Campbell, *Indicative Mood*, 139–51.

encoding the spatial value of remoteness. Thus, the aorist tense-form is perfective in aspect, with the spatial value of remoteness. These are semantic values that are not cancelable but are expressed pragmatically in a variety of ways in context, which will be explored below.

The future tense-form, however, refers to future time in its every usage and is therefore regarded as a genuine tense; that is, future temporal reference is a semantic feature of the verb alongside perfective aspect. Rather than being semantically aspectual-spatial (as the aorist tense-form is here regarded), the future is semantically aspectual-temporal.

Pragmatics

Narrative Functions

Aorist Tense-Form

In narrative texts, the aorist indicative is most often found in narrative proper. While it is used in discourse and even in offline information, its main function in narrative is to provide the mainline of narrative proper, outlining the skeletal structure of the story, as these examples demonstrate.

> **Luke 1:39–41** Ἀναστᾶσα δὲ Μαριὰμ ἐν ταῖς ἡμέραις ταύταις **ἐπορεύθη** εἰς τὴν ὀρεινὴν μετὰ σπουδῆς εἰς πόλιν Ἰούδα, καὶ **εἰσῆλθεν** εἰς τὸν οἶκον Ζαχαρίου καὶ **ἠσπάσατο** τὴν Ἐλισάβετ. καὶ ἐγένετο ὡς **ἤκουσεν** τὸν ἀσπασμὸν τῆς Μαρίας ἡ Ἐλισάβετ, **ἐσκίρτησεν** τὸ βρέφος ἐν τῇ κοιλίᾳ αὐτῆς, καὶ **ἐπλήσθη** πνεύματος ἁγίου ἡ Ἐλισάβετ.

> *In those days Mary set out and **hurried** to a town in the hill country of Judah, where **she entered** Zechariah's house and **greeted** Elizabeth. When Elizabeth **heard** Mary's greeting, the baby **leaped** inside her, and Elizabeth **was filled** with the Holy Spirit.*

> **John 19:32–34** **ἦλθον** οὖν οἱ στρατιῶται καὶ τοῦ μὲν πρώτου **κατέαξαν** τὰ σκέλη καὶ τοῦ ἄλλου τοῦ συσταυρωθέντος αὐτῷ· ἐπὶ δὲ τὸν Ἰησοῦν ἐλθόντες, ὡς **εἶδον** ἤδη αὐτὸν τεθνηκότα, **οὐ κατέαξαν** αὐτοῦ τὰ σκέλη, ἀλλ᾽ εἷς τῶν στρατιωτῶν λόγχῃ αὐτοῦ τὴν πλευρὰν **ἔνυξεν**, καὶ **ἐξῆλθεν** εὐθὺς αἷμα καὶ ὕδωρ.

> *So the soldiers **came** and **broke** the legs of the first man and of the other one who had been crucified with him. When they came to Jesus, **they did not break** his legs since **they saw** that he was already dead. But one of the soldiers **pierced** his side with a spear, and at once blood and water **came out**.*

Narrative mainline creates a remote-perfective context as the events of the story are presented rapidly in quick succession. As such, the aorist indicative is attracted to that mainline, being a remote-perfective tense-form. It is to be remembered, however, that the mainline function of the aorist tense-form is a pragmatic feature and is therefore cancelable.

Future Tense-Form

The future indicative, however, is most often found in discourse rather than narrative proper. This is no doubt due to its future temporal reference: in narrative, reference to the future is performed most naturally by characters within the narrative and thus within their speech (discourse).

John 16:13–14 ὅταν δὲ ἔλθῃ ἐκεῖνος, τὸ πνεῦμα τῆς ἀληθείας, **ὁδηγήσει** ὑμᾶς ἐν τῇ ἀληθείᾳ πάσῃ· οὐ γὰρ **λαλήσει** ἀφ᾽ ἑαυτοῦ, ἀλλ᾽ ὅσα **ἀκούσει λαλήσει** καὶ τὰ ἐρχόμενα **ἀναγγελεῖ** ὑμῖν. ἐκεῖνος ἐμὲ **δοξάσει**, ὅτι ἐκ τοῦ ἐμοῦ **λήμψεται** καὶ **ἀναγγελεῖ** ὑμῖν.

*When the Spirit of truth comes, he will **guide** you into all the truth. For he will **not speak** on his own, but he will **speak** whatever he hears. He will also **declare** to you what is to come. He will **glorify** me, because he will **take** from what is mine and **declare** it to you."*

Aktionsart Interactions (Aorist Tense-Form)

Aktionsart refers to the way a verb behaves in the text when all features of the language and text bear upon it. There are three main elements that determine a particular verb's *Aktionsart*: semantics, lexeme, and context. Accordingly, there are three steps required in order to ascertain what a verb is doing in the text:

1. Identify the semantic value of the verb
2. Consider the lexeme and its interaction with the semantics
3. Consider the context

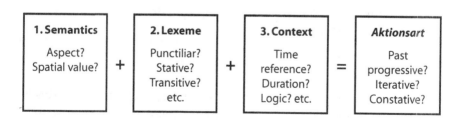

1. Semantics		2. Lexeme		3. Context		Aktionsart
Aspect? Spatial value?	+	Punctiliar? Stative? Transitive? etc.	+	Time reference? Duration? Logic? etc.	=	Past progressive? Iterative? Constative?

There are several ways in which the aorist tense-form functions pragmatically. Below are the most common and important *Aktionsart* descriptions of aorist usage and explanations of how the *Aktionsart* values are arrived at.

Summary

Aorist tense-forms often end up depicting a process or action *in summary*. This is the most common usage of the aorist tense-form and is a natural implicature of perfective aspect. Perfective aspect combines with any lexeme that is not punctiliar or stative to create a summary sense. As long as this summary sense is not overruled by context, the *Aktionsart* is summary.

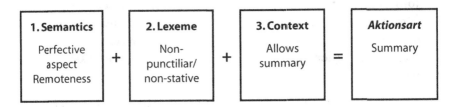

John 1:17 ὅτι ὁ νόμος διὰ Μωϋσέως **ἐδόθη**, ἡ χάρις καὶ ἡ ἀλήθεια διὰ Ἰησοῦ Χριστοῦ **ἐγένετο**.

*... for although the law **was given** through Moses, grace and truth **came** through Jesus Christ.*

John 12:41 ταῦτα **εἶπεν** Ἡσαΐας ὅτι **εἶδεν** τὴν δόξαν αὐτοῦ, καὶ **ἐλάλησεν** περὶ αὐτοῦ.

*Isaiah **said** these things because **he saw** his glory and **spoke** about him.*

Romans 1:21 διότι γνόντες τὸν θεὸν οὐχ ὡς θεὸν **ἐδόξασαν** ἢ **ηὐχαρίστησαν**, ἀλλ᾽ **ἐματαιώθησαν** ἐν τοῖς διαλογισμοῖς αὐτῶν καὶ **ἐσκοτίσθη** ἡ ἀσύνετος αὐτῶν καρδία.

*For though they knew God, **they did not glorify** him as God or **give him thanks**. Instead, their thinking **became futile**, and their senseless minds **were darkened**.*

Punctiliar

Aorist tense-forms sometimes end up depicting a punctiliar action. This is also a natural implicature of perfective aspect. Perfective aspect combines with a punctiliar lexeme to create a punctiliar *Aktionsart*, if this is not overturned by context. A punctiliar lexeme is a word that describes an action that is, by its very nature, once-occurring and instantaneous.

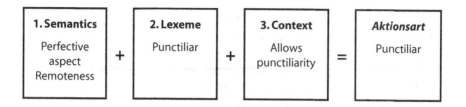

Mark 5:27 ἀκούσασα περὶ τοῦ Ἰησοῦ, ἐλθοῦσα ἐν τῷ ὄχλῳ ὄπισθεν **ἥψατο** τοῦ ἱματίου αὐτοῦ.

*Having heard about Jesus, she came behind him in the crowd and **touched** His robe.*

Mark 14:47 εἷς δέ [τις] τῶν παρεστηκότων σπασάμενος τὴν μάχαιραν **ἔπαισεν** τὸν δοῦλον τοῦ ἀρχιερέως καὶ **ἀφεῖλεν** αὐτοῦ τὸ ὠτάριον.

*And one of those who stood by drew his sword, **struck** the high priest's slave, and **cut off** his ear.*

John 19:34 ἀλλ᾽ εἷς τῶν στρατιωτῶν λόγχῃ αὐτοῦ τὴν πλευρὰν **ἔνυξεν**, καὶ ἐξῆλθεν εὐθὺς αἷμα καὶ ὕδωρ.

*But one of the soldiers **pierced** his side with a spear, and at once blood and water came out.*

Ingressive

Aorist tense-forms are able to depict the entrance into a state or the beginning of a new action. When perfective aspect combines with a stative lexeme, the entrance into the state is in view, thus an ingressive *Aktionsart* is formed. Alternatively, other types of lexemes can form an ingressive sense with perfective aspect due to contextual factors.

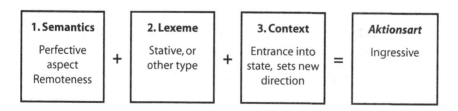

Matthew 22:7 ὁ δὲ βασιλεὺς **ὠργίσθη** καὶ πέμψας τὰ στρατεύματα αὐτοῦ ἀπώλεσεν τοὺς φονεῖς ἐκείνους καὶ τὴν πόλιν αὐτῶν ἐνέπρησεν.

*The king **became angry**, so he sent out his troops, destroyed those murderers, and burned down their city.*

John 12:9 Ἔγνω οὖν [ὁ] ὄχλος πολὺς ἐκ τῶν Ἰουδαίων ὅτι ἐκεῖ ἐστιν καὶ ἦλθον οὐ διὰ τὸν Ἰησοῦν μόνον, ἀλλ᾽ ἵνα καὶ τὸν Λάζαρον ἴδωσιν ὃν ἤγειρεν ἐκ νεκρῶν.

*Then a large crowd of the Jews **learned** he was there. They came not only because of Jesus but also to see Lazarus, the one he had raised from the dead.*

Revelation 20:4 καὶ **ἔζησαν** καὶ ἐβασίλευσαν μετὰ τοῦ Χριστοῦ χίλια ἔτη.

*They **came to life** and reigned with the Christ for 1,000 years.*

Gnomic

Aorist tense-forms can depict gnomic actions, which are universal and timeless. A gnomic *Aktionsart* is created through the combination of perfective aspect and a context in which generic statements are made. These may involve any type of lexeme. Gnomic aorists are not just found in timeless contexts—they are often best translated as present in temporal reference. As such, the gnomic aorist provides a perfective aspect option for the presentation of events that are present in temporal reference in contrast to the (imperfective) present tense-form.

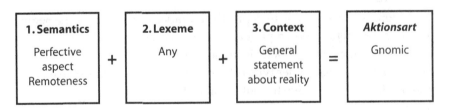

Matthew 23:2 λέγων· ἐπὶ τῆς Μωϋσέως καθέδρας **ἐκάθισαν** οἱ γραμματεῖς καὶ οἱ Φαρισαῖοι.

*The scribes and the Pharisees **sit** in the chair of Moses.*

Luke 7:35 καὶ **ἐδικαιώθη** ἡ σοφία ἀπὸ πάντων τῶν τέκνων αὐτῆς.

*Yet wisdom **is vindicated** by all her children.*

James 1:11 **ἀνέτειλεν** γὰρ ὁ ἥλιος σὺν τῷ καύσωνι καὶ **ἐξήρανεν** τὸν χόρτον καὶ τὸ ἄνθος αὐτοῦ **ἐξέπεσεν** καὶ ἡ εὐπρέπεια τοῦ προσώπου αὐτοῦ **ἀπώλετο**· οὕτως καὶ ὁ πλούσιος ἐν ταῖς πορείαις αὐτοῦ μαρανθήσεται.

*For the sun **rises** with its scorching heat and **dries up** the grass; its flower **falls off**, and its beautiful appearance **is destroyed**. In the same way, the rich man will wither away while pursuing his activities.*

Present Aorist

Though rare in the New Testament, the aorist tense-form can refer to the present even when not in a gnomic usage. In such cases, the aorist provides a perfective option for the depiction of actions that are present in temporal reference. These may involve any type of lexeme, while the present temporal reference is set by the context.

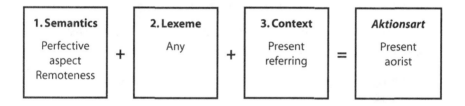

Mark 1:11 καὶ φωνὴ ἐγένετο ἐκ τῶν οὐρανῶν· σὺ εἶ ὁ υἱός μου ὁ ἀγαπητός, ἐν σοὶ **εὐδόκησα**.

*And a voice came from heaven, "You are my beloved Son; with you **I am well pleased**."*

Luke 1:47 καὶ **ἠγαλλίασεν** τὸ πνεῦμά μου ἐπὶ τῷ θεῷ τῷ σωτῆρί μου.

*... and my spirit **rejoices** in God my Savior.*

John 13:31 Ὅτε οὖν ἐξῆλθεν, λέγει Ἰησοῦς· νῦν **ἐδοξάσθη** ὁ υἱὸς τοῦ ἀνθρώπου καὶ ὁ θεὸς **ἐδοξάσθη** ἐν αὐτῷ.

*When he had gone out, Jesus said, "Now the Son of Man **is glorified**, and God **is glorified** in him."*

Future Aorist

More commonly, the aorist tense-form may be used in future-referring contexts. The difference between the future-referring aorist and the future tense-form may be seen in the fact that the aorist semantically encodes remoteness. This remoteness accounts for one of the common ways in which the aorist refers to the future, which is within future conditional sentences. In such cases, remoteness functions logically and contributes to the contingency inherent to such conditions. Future aorists may involve any type of lexeme, while the future temporal reference is set by the context.

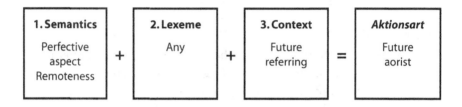

Mark 11:24 διὰ τοῦτο λέγω ὑμῖν, πάντα ὅσα προσεύχεσθε καὶ αἰτεῖσθε, πιστεύετε ὅτι **ἐλάβετε**, καὶ ἔσται ὑμῖν.

Therefore, I tell you, all the things you pray and ask for — believe that **you will receive** *them, and you will have them.*

Luke 17:6 εἶπεν δὲ ὁ κύριος· εἰ ἔχετε πίστιν ὡς κόκκον σινάπεως, ἐλέγετε ἂν τῇ συκαμίνῳ [ταύτῃ]· ἐκριζώθητι καὶ φυτεύθητι ἐν τῇ θαλάσσῃ· καὶ **ὑπήκουσεν** ἂν ὑμῖν.

"If you have faith the size of a mustard seed" the Lord said, "you can say to this mulberry tree, 'Be uprooted and planted in the sea,' and **it will obey** *you."*

Revelation 10:7 ἀλλ' ἐν ταῖς ἡμέραις τῆς φωνῆς τοῦ ἑβδόμου ἀγγέλου, ὅταν μέλλῃ σαλπίζειν, καὶ **ἐτελέσθη** τὸ μυστήριον τοῦ θεοῦ, ὡς εὐηγγέλισεν τοὺς ἑαυτοῦ δούλους τοὺς προφήτας.

… but in the days of the sound of the seventh angel, when he will blow his trumpet, then God's hidden plan **will be completed**, *as he announced to his servants the prophets.*

Nonindicative Usage (Aorist Tense-Form)

Subjunctive Mood

Verbal aspect is fully operational within the subjunctive mood. The use of the aorist subjunctive reveals regular expressions of perfective aspect; activities are summarized, punctiliar, or concrete rather than abstract.[2] These examples demonstrate the external viewpoint of the perfective aspect conveyed by the aorist subjunctive—the actions are portrayed as a whole.

Luke 24:49 καὶ [ἰδοὺ] ἐγὼ ἀποστέλλω τὴν ἐπαγγελίαν τοῦ πατρός μου ἐφ᾽ ὑμᾶς· ὑμεῖς δὲ καθίσατε ἐν τῇ πόλει ἕως οὗ **ἐνδύσησθε** ἐξ ὕψους δύναμιν.

*And look, I am sending you what my Father promised. As for you, stay in the city until **you are empowered** from on high.*

John 12:49 ὅτι ἐγὼ ἐξ ἐμαυτοῦ οὐκ ἐλάλησα, ἀλλ᾽ ὁ πέμψας με πατὴρ αὐτός μοι ἐντολὴν δέδωκεν τί **εἴπω** καὶ τί **λαλήσω**.

*For I have not spoken on my own, but the father himself who sent me has given me a command as to what **I should say** and what **I should speak**.*

2 Corinthians 9:4 μή πως ἐὰν **ἔλθωσιν** σὺν ἐμοὶ Μακεδόνες καὶ **εὕρωσιν** ὑμᾶς ἀπαρασκευάστους **καταισχυνθῶμεν** ἡμεῖς, ἵνα μὴ λέγω ὑμεῖς, ἐν τῇ ὑποστάσει ταύτῃ.

*For if any Macedonians **should come** with me and **find** you unprepared, we—not to mention you—**would be embarrassed** by this confidence.*

The aorist subjunctive is found within certain constructions that do not normally employ the present subjunctive. The emphatic future negative construction is one that is only ever found with the aorist subjunctive (and also the future indicative). This is due to the fact that perfective aspect is needed when speaking of events that will *not* occur in the future.[3] We thus observe a parallel between the aorist subjunctive and the future indicative, since both verbs encode perfective aspect.

---

2. Campbell, *Non-Indicative Verbs*, 56.
3. This is a complicated concept; to follow it up see Campbell, *Non-Indicative Verbs*, 58–59.

John 8:12 Πάλιν οὖν αὐτοῖς ἐλάλησεν ὁ Ἰησοῦς λέγων· ἐγώ εἰμι τὸ φῶς τοῦ κόσμου· ὁ ἀκολουθῶν ἐμοὶ **οὐ μὴ περιπατήσῃ** ἐν τῇ σκοτίᾳ, ἀλλ᾽ ἕξει τὸ φῶς τῆς ζωῆς.

*Then Jesus spoke to them again: "I am the light of the world. Anyone who follows me **will never walk** in the darkness but will have the light of life."*

Romans 4:8 μακάριος ἀνὴρ οὗ **οὐ μὴ λογίσηται** κύριος ἁμαρτίαν.

*How happy the man whom the Lord **will never charge** with sin!*

Another construction that employs only the aorist subjunctive and never the present subjunctive is ἕως + *subjunctive*. Perfective aspect is suited to this usage since this construction often indicates a point in the future at which a new situation is inaugurated or an existing situation is brought to an end.

Luke 24:49 καὶ [ἰδοὺ] ἐγὼ ἀποστέλλω τὴν ἐπαγγελίαν τοῦ πατρός μου ἐφ᾽ ὑμᾶς· ὑμεῖς δὲ καθίσατε ἐν τῇ πόλει **ἕως** οὗ **ἐνδύσησθε** ἐξ ὕψους δύναμιν.

*And look, I am sending you what my Father promised. As for you, stay in the city **until you are empowered** from on high.*

Acts 2:35 **ἕως** ἂν **θῶ** τοὺς ἐχθρούς σου ὑποπόδιον τῶν ποδῶν σου.

*... **until I make** your enemies your footstool.*

Imperative Mood

The aorist imperative semantically encodes perfective aspect. Its main pragmatic function is to convey *specific* commands. A command is specific if the situation in which it is to be carried out is specific; it involves a specific agent performing action within a specific situation. This function of the aorist imperative contrasts clearly with the present imperative, which normally conveys commands that are general in nature. Perfective aspect is ideal for the communication of specific instruction, since the external viewpoint lends itself to the expression of definiteness.

It is to be remembered that specific instruction is a pragmatic function of aorist imperatives. There will be cases in which specific instruction is clearly not intended, and this is to be evaluated according to context. In such cases, the aorist imperative may express general instruction, which is viewed as a whole because of its perfective aspect. When context makes it clear that this is how the aorist imperative is operating, there is little that distinguishes it from the normal function of the present imperative.[4]

To suggest that the aorist imperative conveys specific instruction does not imply that the intended action is to be *instantaneous* or *immediate* in nature. Such a conclusion would be to confuse aspect with *Aktionsart* in similar manner to the mistake of concluding that the aorist indicative must always implicate punctiliar action, which it does not. Thus the aorist imperative issues a specific command, but not necessarily an *instantaneous* command. The examples below demonstrate specific instructions issued with the aorist imperative.

Luke 5:4 Ὡς δὲ ἐπαύσατο λαλῶν, εἶπεν πρὸς τὸν Σίμωνα· **ἐπανάγαγε** εἰς τὸ βάθος καὶ **χαλάσατε** τὰ δίκτυα ὑμῶν εἰς ἄγραν.

*When he had finished speaking, he said to Simon, "**Put out** into deep water and **let down** your nets for a catch."*

John 2:7–8 λέγει αὐτοῖς ὁ Ἰησοῦς· **γεμίσατε** τὰς ὑδρίας ὕδατος. καὶ ἐγέμισαν αὐτὰς ἕως ἄνω. καὶ λέγει αὐτοῖς· **ἀντλήσατε** νῦν καὶ φέρετε τῷ ἀρχιτρικλίνῳ· οἱ δὲ ἤνεγκαν.

*"**Fill** the jars with water," Jesus told them. So they filled them to the brim. Then he said to them, "Now **draw some out** and take it to the chief servant." And they did.*

John 19:6 Ὅτε οὖν εἶδον αὐτὸν οἱ ἀρχιερεῖς καὶ οἱ ὑπηρέται ἐκραύγασαν λέγοντες· **σταύρωσον σταύρωσον**. λέγει αὐτοῖς ὁ Πιλᾶτος· **λάβετε** αὐτὸν ὑμεῖς καὶ **σταυρώσατε**· ἐγὼ γὰρ οὐχ εὑρίσκω ἐν αὐτῷ αἰτίαν.

*When the chief priests and the temple police saw him, they shouted, "**Crucify! Crucify!**" Pilate responded, "**Take** him and **crucify** him yourselves, for I find no grounds for charging him."*

There are, however, instances where it is difficult ascribing this function to aorist imperatives. It is to be remembered at this point that the indication of specific commands is a pragmatic function of the aorist imperative and is therefore cancelable. In such cases, the semantic value of perfective aspect is to understood to be pragmatically functioning in some other way.

---

4. For more on nonspecific aorist imperatives, see Campbell, *Non-Indicative Verbs*, 86–91.

Participle

The aorist participle semantically encodes perfective aspect. It is its aspect that leads to the aorist participle's main pragmatic function in which it most often expresses action that is antecedent to its leading verb. That is, the action of the leading verb occurs *after* the action of the aorist participle.

> **Matthew 5:1** Ἰδὼν δὲ τοὺς ὄχλους ἀνέβη εἰς τὸ ὄρος, καὶ **καθίσαντος** αὐτοῦ προσῆλθαν αὐτῷ οἱ μαθηταὶ αὐτοῦ.
>
> *After he saw the crowds, he went up on the mountain, and **after he sat down**, his disciples came to him.*

> **John 19:29–30** σκεῦος ἔκειτο ὄξους μεστόν· σπόγγον οὖν μεστὸν τοῦ ὄξους ὑσσώπῳ **περιθέντες** προσήνεγκαν αὐτοῦ τῷ στόματι. ὅτε οὖν ἔλαβεν τὸ ὄξος [ὁ] Ἰησοῦς εἶπεν· τετέλεσται, καὶ **κλίνας** τὴν κεφαλὴν παρέδωκεν τὸ πνεῦμα.
>
> *A jar full of sour wine was sitting there; so **after they fixed** a sponge full of sour wine on hyssop they held it up to his mouth. When Jesus had received the sour wine, he said, "It is finished!" Then **after bowing** his head, he gave up his spirit.*

> **Romans 5:1** **Δικαιωθέντες** οὖν ἐκ πίστεως εἰρήνην ἔχομεν πρὸς τὸν θεὸν διὰ τοῦ κυρίου ἡμῶν Ἰησοῦ Χριστοῦ.
>
> *Therefore, **since we have been declared righteous** by faith, we have peace with God through our Lord Jesus Christ.*

The perfective aspect of the aorist participle enables it to express action that is temporally subsequent to its leading verb, though this is rare.

> **Acts 25:13** Ἡμερῶν δὲ διαγενομένων τινῶν Ἀγρίππας ὁ βασιλεὺς καὶ Βερνίκη κατήντησαν εἰς Καισάρειαν **ἀσπασάμενοι** τὸν Φῆστον.
>
> *After some days had passed, King Agrippa and Bernice arrived in Caesarea and **greeted** Festus.*

Furthermore, the aorist participle is capable of expressing action that is contemporaneous to the action of the main verb. This, however, occurs only within constructions of attendant circumstance, which will be dealt with later. Suffice to say, the perfective aspect of the aorist participle issues a different pragmatic usage in such constructions.

Luke 1:19 καὶ **ἀποκριθεὶς** ὁ ἄγγελος εἶπεν αὐτῷ· ἐγώ εἰμι Γαβριὴλ ὁ παρεστηκὼς ἐνώπιον τοῦ θεοῦ καὶ ἀπεστάλην λαλῆσαι πρὸς σὲ καὶ εὐαγγελίσασθαί σοι ταῦτα.

*The angel **answered** and said to him, "I am Gabriel, who stands in the presence of God, and I was sent to speak to you and tell you this good news."*

Infinitive

Though difficult to appreciate at times, aorist infinitives semantically encode perfective aspect. This aspect is pragmatically expressed in a variety of ways, with the primary function to be found within particular infinitival constructions: the usage of the aorist infinitive is mostly determined through infinitival constructions that commonly require it. For many of these constructions, the preference for the aorist infinitive is clearly due to its perfective aspect.

Three of these constructions are related to temporal expression—one expressing antecedent time, and two expressing subsequent time. These are μετὰ τό + *infinitive*, πρὸ τοῦ + *infinitive*, and πρίν + *infinitive* respectively. The perfective aspect of the aorist infinitive allows its usage in these temporal constructions that indicate antecedent and subsequent action. In a manner similar to that of the aorist participle, the undefined and summary viewpoint of the perfective aspect of the aorist infinitive naturally suits the depiction of action occuring *either side* of the leading verb, temporally speaking.

Luke 12:5 ὑποδείξω δὲ ὑμῖν τίνα φοβηθῆτε· φοβήθητε τὸν **μετὰ τὸ ἀποκτεῖναι** ἔχοντα ἐξουσίαν ἐμβαλεῖν εἰς τὴν γέενναν. ναὶ λέγω ὑμῖν, τοῦτον φοβήθητε.

*But I will warn you whom you should fear: fear him who, **after he has killed**, has authority to cast into hell. Yes, I tell you, fear him!*

Luke 22:15 καὶ εἶπεν πρὸς αὐτούς· ἐπιθυμίᾳ ἐπεθύμησα τοῦτο τὸ πάσχα φαγεῖν μεθ᾽ ὑμῶν **πρὸ τοῦ με παθεῖν.**

*And he said to them, "I have eagerly desired to eat this Passover with you **before I suffer.**"*

John 4:49 λέγει πρὸς αὐτὸν ὁ βασιλικός· κύριε, κατάβηθι **πρὶν ἀποθανεῖν** τὸ παιδίον μου.

*The official said to him, "Sir, come down **before my child dies.**"*

Aktionsart Interactions (Future Tense-Form)

There are several ways in which the future tense-form functions pragmatically. Below are the most common and important *Aktionsart* descriptions of future usage and explanations of how the *Aktionsart* values are arrived at. It will be noticed that these *Aktionsarten* are parallel to those found in aorist usage. This is to be expected, given their sharing of perfective aspect.

Summary Future

Future tense-forms often end up depicting a process or action *in summary*. This is the most common usage of the future tense-form and is a natural implicature of perfective aspect. Perfective aspect combines with any lexeme that is not punctiliar or stative to create a summary sense. As long as this summary sense is not overruled by context, the *Aktionsart* is summary.

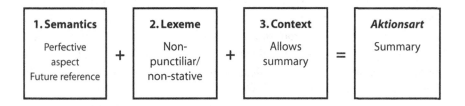

Matthew 10:21 Παραδώσει δὲ ἀδελφὸς ἀδελφὸν εἰς θάνατον καὶ πατὴρ τέκνον, καὶ **ἐπαναστήσονται** τέκνα ἐπὶ γονεῖς καὶ **θανατώσουσιν** αὐτούς.

*"Brother **will betray** brother to death, and a father his child. Children will even **rise up** against their parents and **will put them to death**."*

Luke 13:24 ἀγωνίζεσθε εἰσελθεῖν διὰ τῆς στενῆς θύρας, ὅτι πολλοί, λέγω ὑμῖν, **ζητήσουσιν** εἰσελθεῖν καὶ **οὐκ ἰσχύσουσιν**.

*Make every effort to enter through the narrow door, because I tell you, many **will try** to enter and **won't be able**.*

John 16:13–14 ὅταν δὲ ἔλθῃ ἐκεῖνος, τὸ πνεῦμα τῆς ἀληθείας, **ὁδηγήσει** ὑμᾶς ἐν τῇ ἀληθείᾳ πάσῃ· **οὐ** γὰρ **λαλήσει** ἀφ᾽ ἑαυτοῦ, ἀλλ᾽ ὅσα **ἀκούσει λαλήσει** καὶ τὰ ἐρχόμενα **ἀναγγελεῖ** ὑμῖν. ἐκεῖνος ἐμὲ **δοξάσει**, ὅτι ἐκ τοῦ ἐμοῦ **λήμψεται** καὶ **ἀναγγελεῖ** ὑμῖν.

*When the Spirit of truth comes, **he will guide** you into all the truth. For **he will not speak** on his own, but **he will speak** whatever **he hears**. He will also **declare** to you what is to come. He **will glorify** me, because **he will take** from what is mine and **declare** it to you.*

Punctiliar

Future tense-forms sometimes end up depicting a punctiliar action. This is also a natural implicature of perfective aspect. Perfective aspect combines with a punctiliar lexeme to create a punctiliar *Aktionsart*, if this is not overturned by context. A punctiliar lexeme is a word that describes an action that is, by its very nature, once-occurring and instantaneous.

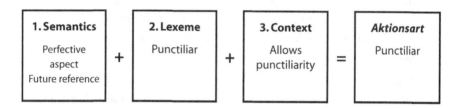

Mark 14:27 καὶ λέγει αὐτοῖς ὁ Ἰησοῦς ὅτι πάντες σκανδαλισθήσεσθε, ὅτι γέγραπται· **πατάξω** τὸν ποιμένα, καὶ τὰ πρόβατα διασκορπισθήσονται.

*Then Jesus said to them, "All of you will run away, because it is written: 'I **will strike** the shepherd, and the sheep will be scattered.' "*

Luke 5:37 καὶ οὐδεὶς βάλλει οἶνον νέον εἰς ἀσκοὺς παλαιούς· εἰ δὲ μή γε, **ῥήξει** ὁ οἶνος ὁ νέος τοὺς ἀσκοὺς καὶ αὐτὸς ἐκχυθήσεται καὶ οἱ ἀσκοὶ ἀπολοῦνται.

*And no one puts new wine into old wineskins. Otherwise, the new wine **will burst** the skins, it will spill, and the skins will be ruined.*

Acts 1:5 ὅτι Ἰωάννης μὲν ἐβάπτισεν ὕδατι, ὑμεῖς δὲ ἐν πνεύματι **βαπτισθήσεσθε** ἁγίῳ οὐ μετὰ πολλὰς ταύτας ἡμέρας.

*… for John baptized with water, but you **will be baptized** with the Holy Spirit not many days from now.*

Ingressive

As with the aorist tense-form, the future tense-form is able to depict ingressive actions, in which the beginning of a state or action is in view.

This occurs when the perfective aspect of the future form combines with stative lexemes, or when the context denotes a new situation that signals the beginning of the action.

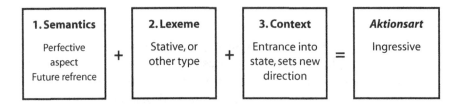

Matthew 9:18   Ταῦτα αὐτοῦ λαλοῦντος αὐτοῖς, ἰδοὺ ἄρχων εἷς ἐλθὼν προσεκύνει αὐτῷ λέγων ὅτι ἡ θυγάτηρ μου ἄρτι ἐτελεύτησεν· ἀλλὰ ἐλθὼν ἐπίθες τὴν χεῖρά σου ἐπ᾽ αὐτήν, καὶ **ζήσεται**.

*While he was saying these things to them, suddenly a synagogue leader came and knelt before him, saying, "My daughter has just died; but come and lay your hand on her, and **she will live**."*

Matthew 19:21   ἔφη αὐτῷ ὁ Ἰησοῦς· εἰ θέλεις τέλειος εἶναι, ὕπαγε πώλησόν σου τὰ ὑπάρχοντα καὶ δὸς [τοῖς] πτωχοῖς, καὶ **ἕξεις** θησαυρὸν ἐν οὐρανοῖς, καὶ δεῦρο ἀκολούθει μοι.

*Jesus said to him, "If you want to be perfect, go, sell your possessions and give to the poor, and **you will have** treasure in heaven; then come, follow me."*

Mark 4:13   Καὶ λέγει αὐτοῖς· οὐκ οἴδατε τὴν παραβολὴν ταύτην, καὶ πῶς πάσας τὰς παραβολὰς **γνώσεσθε**;

*And he said to them, "Do you not understand this parable? How then **will you understand** all the parables?"*

Exercises for Aorist and Future Tense-Forms

For each passage, (1) write about the semantic meaning of the verb, (2) state the contribution of the lexeme, and (3) discuss the function of the verb in context. Once you have written your answers, summarize your findings in the boxes below each passage.

Example:

John 19:34 ἀλλ᾽ εἷς τῶν στρατιωτῶν λόγχῃ αὐτοῦ τὴν πλευρὰν **ἔνυξεν**, καὶ ἐξῆλθεν εὐθὺς αἷμα καὶ ὕδωρ.

*But one of the soldiers **pierced** his side with a spear, and at once blood and water came out.*

1. Semantic meaning of the verb. The aorist indicative semantically encodes perfective aspect and the spatial value of remoteness.
2. Contribution of the lexeme. The lexeme is punctiliar; it is an instantaneous action.
3. Function in context. The context allows punctiliarity.

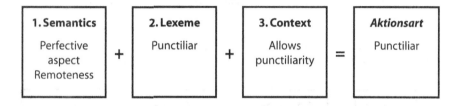

John 7:32 **ἤκουσαν** οἱ Φαρισαῖοι τοῦ ὄχλου γογγύζοντος περὶ αὐτοῦ ταῦτα, καὶ **ἀπέστειλαν** οἱ ἀρχιερεῖς καὶ οἱ Φαρισαῖοι ὑπηρέτας ἵνα πιάσωσιν αὐτόν.

*The Pharisees **heard** the crowd muttering these things about him, so the chief priests and the Pharisees **sent** temple police to arrest him.*

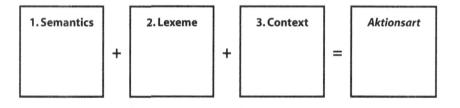

Romans 6:14 ἁμαρτία γὰρ ὑμῶν **οὐ κυριεύσει·** οὐ γάρ ἐστε ὑπὸ νόμον ἀλλὰ ὑπὸ χάριν.

*For sin **will not rule** over you, because you are not under law but under grace.*

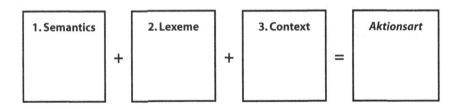

Romans 3:23 πάντες γὰρ **ἥμαρτον** καὶ ὑστεροῦνται τῆς δόξης τοῦ θεοῦ.

*For all **have sinned** and fall short of the glory of God.*

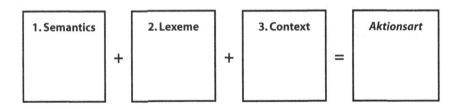

John 1:10 ἐν τῷ κόσμῳ ἦν, καὶ ὁ κόσμος δι᾽ αὐτοῦ ἐγένετο, καὶ ὁ κόσμος αὐτὸν **οὐκ ἔγνω.**

*He was in the world, and the world was created through him, yet the world **did not recognize** him.*

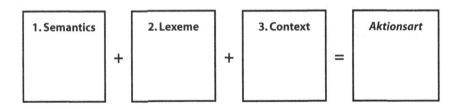

Mark 14:27 καὶ λέγει αὐτοῖς ὁ Ἰησοῦς ὅτι πάντες σκανδαλισθήσεσθε, ὅτι γέγραπται· **πατάξω** τὸν ποιμένα, καὶ τὰ πρόβατα διασκορπισθήσονται.

Then Jesus said to them, "All of you will run away, because it is written: 'I will strike the shepherd, and the sheep will be scattered.' "

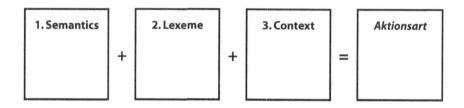

John 7:26 καὶ ἴδε παρρησίᾳ λαλεῖ καὶ οὐδὲν αὐτῷ λέγουσιν. μήποτε ἀληθῶς **ἔγνωσαν** οἱ ἄρχοντες ὅτι οὗτός ἐστιν ὁ χριστός;

Yet, look! he's speaking publicly and they're saying nothing to him. Can it be true that the authorities know he is the Christ?

1. Semantics		2. Lexeme		3. Context		Aktionsart
	+		+		=	

Romans 8:11 εἰ δὲ τὸ πνεῦμα τοῦ ἐγείραντος τὸν Ἰησοῦν ἐκ νεκρῶν οἰκεῖ ἐν ὑμῖν, ὁ ἐγείρας Χριστὸν ἐκ νεκρῶν **ζῳοποιήσει** καὶ τὰ θνητὰ σώματα ὑμῶν διὰ τοῦ ἐνοικοῦντος αὐτοῦ πνεύματος ἐν ὑμῖν.

And if the Spirit of him who raised Jesus from the dead lives in you, then he who raised Christ from the dead will also bring your mortal bodies to life through his Spirit who lives in you.

1. Semantics		2. Lexeme		3. Context		Aktionsart
	+		+		=	

Romans 8:30 οὓς δὲ **προώρισεν**, τούτους καὶ **ἐκάλεσεν·** καὶ οὓς **ἐκάλεσεν**, τούτους καὶ **ἐδικαίωσεν·** οὓς δὲ **ἐδικαίωσεν**, τούτους καὶ **ἐδόξασεν**.

*And those **he predestines**, he also **calls**; and those **he calls**, he also justifies; and those **he justifies**, he also **glorifies**.*

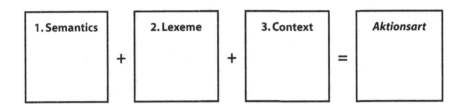

Chapter 9

Perfect and Pluperfect Tense-Forms

—〜〜—

Semantics
Verbal Aspect
The verbal aspect of the perfect tense-form is a matter of debate, with options ranging from stative, perfective, and imperfective, or both perfective and imperfective. In part, this confusion stems from the assumption that the perfect in Greek is similar to that in Latin. Nevertheless, regarding the perfect as encoding imperfective aspect provides the best power of explanation and therefore is the position adopted here.[1]

The perfect and pluperfect tense-forms encode imperfective aspect at the semantic level. Imperfective aspect views an action or state from the inside; it is the internal viewpoint. Using the illustration of the reporter and the street parade, the internal viewpoint is the view from the street, with the parade unfolding in full view. Unlike the view from afar (in the helicopter = perfective aspect), the reporter on the street does not view the beginning or end of the parade, but has a view of the details.

Spatial Qualities
Since the perfect and pluperfect tense-forms are here regarded as imperfective in aspect, the question must be raised as to how they are to be distinguished from the present and imperfect tense-forms. Just as the present and imperfect tense-forms semantically encode the spatial values

---

1. For extensive argumentation along such lines, see Campbell, *Indicative Mood*, 184–89.

of proximity and remoteness respectively, so too the perfect and pluperfect encodes these values respectively.

For these forms, however, the spatial values are heightened. Thus, the perfect tense-form semantically encodes imperfective aspect with the spatial value of heightened proximity. The pluperfect tense-form semantically encodes imperfective aspect with the spatial value of heightened remoteness. The diagram below demonstrates the difference between proximity (present tense-form) and heightened proximity (perfect tense-form).

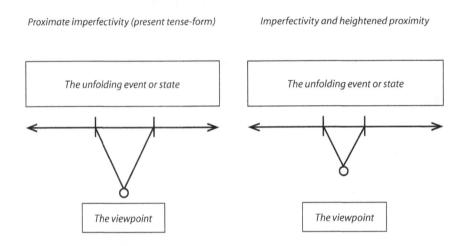

Proximate imperfectivity (present tense-form)   *Imperfectivity and heightened proximity*

Pragmatics
Narrative Functions
Perfect Tense-Form

In narrative texts, the perfect indicative is most often found in discourse—direct discourse, indirect discourse, and authorial discourse, as illustrated by these examples. In this way, the distribution of the perfect parallels that of the present.

> **John 7:28** ἔκραξεν οὖν ἐν τῷ ἱερῷ διδάσκων ὁ Ἰησοῦς καὶ λέγων· κἀμὲ **οἴδατε** καὶ **οἴδατε** πόθεν εἰμί· καὶ ἀπ᾽ ἐμαυτοῦ **οὐκ ἐλήλυθα**, ἀλλ᾽ ἔστιν ἀληθινὸς ὁ πέμψας με, ὃν ὑμεῖς **οὐκ οἴδατε**.

> *As he was teaching in the temple complex, Jesus cried out, "**You know** me and **you know** where I am from. Yet I **have not come** on my own, but the One who sent me is true. **You don't know** him."*

John 15:24 εἰ τὰ ἔργα μὴ ἐποίησα ἐν αὐτοῖς ἃ οὐδεὶς ἄλλος ἐποίησεν· ἁμαρτίαν οὐκ εἴχοσαν· νῦν δὲ καὶ **ἑωράκασιν** καὶ **μεμισήκασιν** καὶ ἐμὲ καὶ τὸν πατέρα μου.

*If I had not done the works among them that no one else has done, they would not have sin. Now **they see** and **hate** both me and my Father.*

Discourse creates a proximate-imperfective context as the speech or thought is presented immediately before the reader's eyes, as though unfolding. As such, the perfect indicative is attracted to discourse, being a proximate-imperfective tense-form. It is to be remembered, however, that the discourse function of the perfect tense-form is a pragmatic feature and is therefore cancelable.

Pluperfect Tense-Form

The pluperfect indicative, however, is most often found in narrative proper rather than discourse. Its normal function within narrative proper is to provide offline material. While aorists typically provide the skeletal structure of the narrative mainline, pluperfects most often provide supplementary information that describes, characterizes, or explains, as illustrated by these examples. In this way, the distribution of pluperfects parallels that of the imperfect.

Luke 4:41 ἐξήρχετο δὲ καὶ δαιμόνια ἀπὸ πολλῶν κρ[αυγ]άζοντα καὶ λέγοντα ὅτι σὺ εἶ ὁ υἱὸς τοῦ θεοῦ. καὶ ἐπιτιμῶν οὐκ εἴα αὐτὰ λαλεῖν, ὅτι **ᾔδεισαν** τὸν χριστὸν αὐτὸν εἶναι.

*Also, demons were coming out of many, shouting and saying, "You are the Son of God!" But he rebuked them and would not allow them to speak, because **they knew** he was the Christ.*

John 7:30 Ἐζήτουν οὖν αὐτὸν πιάσαι, καὶ οὐδεὶς ἐπέβαλεν ἐπ᾽ αὐτὸν τὴν χεῖρα, ὅτι **οὔπω ἐληλύθει** ἡ ὥρα αὐτοῦ.

*Then they tried to seize him. Yet no one laid a hand on him because his hour **had not yet come**.*

Offline material is inherently remote-imperfective in nature, as the supplementary information provides an internal view (imperfective), but this is not presented as being immediately before the reader's eyes. It supplements the remote mainline and thus is remote in nature. As such, the pluperfect indicative is attracted to offline material, since it is a remote-imperfective tense-form. It is to be remembered, however, that the offline function of the pluperfect tense-form is a pragmatic feature and is therefore cancelable.

Aktionsart Interactions (Perfect Tense-Form)

Aktionsart refers to the way a verb behaves in the text when all features of the language and text bear upon it. There are three main elements that determine a particular verb's *Aktionsart*: semantics, lexeme, and context. Accordingly, there are three steps required in order to ascertain what a verb is doing in the text:

1. Identify the semantic value of the verb
2. Consider the lexeme, and its interaction with the semantics
3. Consider the context

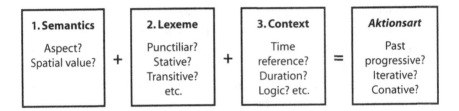

The word "have" in translation of perfects comes from the traditional understanding of the perfect, in which the verb was understood as conveying a past action with present consequence. While rendering the perfect will occasionally require the word "have" in our translations, this should not be supplied by default. Context will determine whether "have" needs to be included in our translation. Perfects will normally refer either to the present (e.g., stative perfects) or to the past (e.g., historical perfects), and as such the "have" translation will only be required in certain circumstances.

There are several ways in which the perfect tense-form functions pragmatically. Below are the most common and important *Aktionsart* descriptions of perfect usage and explanations of how the *Aktionsart* values are arrived at.

Stative

Perfect tense-forms often end up depicting a state. This is also a natural implicature of imperfective aspect. Imperfective aspect combines with a stative lexeme to create a stative *Aktionsart*, if this is not overturned by context. A stative lexeme is a word that describes a state of being rather than a process or transitive action. Sometimes the context can create a stative *Aktionsart* even if the lexeme is not in itself stative. Stative perfects are normally present in their temporal reference.

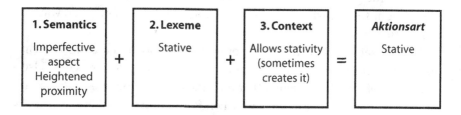

Mark 1:15 καὶ λέγων ὅτι **πεπλήρωται** ὁ καιρὸς καὶ **ἤγγικεν** ἡ βασιλεία τοῦ θεοῦ· μετανοεῖτε καὶ πιστεύετε ἐν τῷ εὐαγγελίῳ.

*... and saying, "The time **is fulfilled**, and the kingdom of God **is near**. Repent and believe in the good news!"*

John 7:28 ἔκραξεν οὖν ἐν τῷ ἱερῷ διδάσκων ὁ Ἰησοῦς καὶ λέγων· κἀμὲ **οἴδατε** καὶ **οἴδατε** πόθεν εἰμί· καὶ ἀπ᾽ ἐμαυτοῦ οὐκ ἐλήλυθα, ἀλλ᾽ ἔστιν ἀληθινὸς ὁ πέμψας με, ὃν ὑμεῖς **οὐκ οἴδατε**.

*As he was teaching in the temple complex, Jesus cried out, "**You know** me and **you know** where I am from. Yet I have not come on my own, but the one who sent me is true. You **don't know** him."*

John 11:27 λέγει αὐτῷ· ναὶ κύριε, ἐγὼ **πεπίστευκα** ὅτι σὺ εἶ ὁ χριστὸς ὁ υἱὸς τοῦ θεοῦ ὁ εἰς τὸν κόσμον ἐρχόμενος.

*"Yes, Lord," she told him, "**I believe** you are the Christ, the Son of God, the One coming into the world."*

Historical Perfect

The perfect tense-form is often used in nonpresent contexts, most often past-referring. These are best translated like aorists, though are not the same as aorists in meaning. There are two basic types of historical perfects: those that introduce discourse and those that employ lexemes of propulsion. In this way, the historical perfect parallels the historical present almost exactly; the same functions are observed with the same group of lexemes.

First, the historical perfects that introduce discourse utilize the perfect tense-form because they are leading into a proximate-imperfective context (discourse). In such cases, the proximate-imperfective nature of discourse "spills over" onto the verb that introduces it.

Second, lexemes of propulsion are verbs that convey transition—the movement from one point to another. These include verbs of coming and going, lifting, taking, giving, and so on. The proximate-imperfective nature of the perfect tense-form combines with these lexemes in order to highlight the transition that is conveyed. There is no obvious way to convey this in translation.

One caveat to note is that verbs of propulsion do not necessarily form historical perfects. As with the historical present, such lexemes may also be used to refer to the present rather than the past. The point is, rather, that these lexemes may refer to the past when found in past contexts.

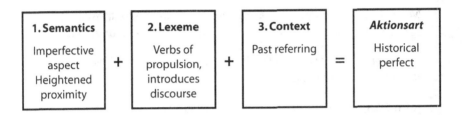

Mark 9:13 ἀλλὰ λέγω ὑμῖν ὅτι καὶ Ἡλίας **ἐλήλυθεν**, καὶ ἐποίησαν αὐτῷ ὅσα ἤθελον, καθὼς γέγραπται ἐπ᾽ αὐτόν.

*But I tell you that Elijah **came**, and they did to him whatever they wanted, just as it is written about him.*

Luke 4:18 πνεῦμα κυρίου ἐπ᾽ ἐμὲ οὗ εἵνεκεν ἔχρισέν με εὐαγγελίσασθαι πτωχοῖς, **ἀπέσταλκέν** με, κηρύξαι αἰχμαλώτοις ἄφεσιν καὶ τυφλοῖς ἀνάβλεψιν, ἀποστεῖλαι τεθραυσμένους ἐν ἀφέσει.

*The Spirit of the Lord is on me, because he anointed me to preach good news to the poor. He **sent** me to proclaim freedom to the captives and recovery of sight to the blind, to set free the oppressed.*

John 1:15 Ἰωάννης μαρτυρεῖ περὶ αὐτοῦ καὶ **κέκραγεν** λέγων· οὗτος ἦν ὃν εἶπον· ὁ ὀπίσω μου ἐρχόμενος ἔμπροσθέν μου γέγονεν, ὅτι πρῶτός μου ἦν.

*John testified concerning him and **exclaimed**, "This was the One of whom I said, 'The One coming after me has surpassed me, because he was before me.'"*

Progressive

Perfect tense-forms sometimes end up depicting a process or action *in progress*. This usage of the perfect tense-form is not widely acknowledged, though is a natural expression of imperfective aspect. Imperfective aspect combines with any lexeme that is not punctiliar or stative to create a progressive sense. As long as this progressive sense is not overruled by context, the *Aktionsart* may be progressive.

A word of caution: sometimes it is difficult to decide whether a perfect is progressive or historical when the context would allow either. Care must be exercised here, as the outcome can be quite different either way.

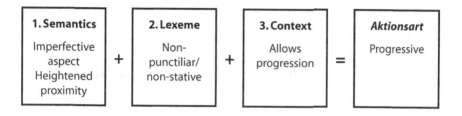

Mark 7:37 καὶ ὑπερπερισσῶς ἐξεπλήσσοντο λέγοντες· καλῶς πάντα **πεποίηκεν**, καὶ τοὺς κωφοὺς ποιεῖ ἀκούειν καὶ [τοὺς] ἀλάλους λαλεῖν.

*They were extremely astonished and said, "**He does** everything well! He even makes deaf people hear, and people unable to speak, talk!"*

John 17:6 Ἐφανέρωσά σου τὸ ὄνομα τοῖς ἀνθρώποις οὓς ἔδωκάς μοι ἐκ τοῦ κόσμου. σοὶ ἦσαν κἀμοὶ αὐτοὺς ἔδωκας καὶ τὸν λόγον σου **τετήρηκαν**.

*I have revealed your name to the men you gave me from the world. They were yours, you gave them to me, and **they keep** your word.*

Acts 21:28 κράζοντες· ἄνδρες Ἰσραηλῖται, βοηθεῖτε· οὗτός ἐστιν ὁ ἄνθρωπος ὁ κατὰ τοῦ λαοῦ καὶ τοῦ νόμου καὶ τοῦ τόπου τούτου πάντας πανταχῇ διδάσκων, ἔτι τε καὶ Ἕλληνας εἰσήγαγεν εἰς τὸ ἱερὸν καὶ **κεκοίνωκεν** τὸν ἅγιον τόπον τοῦτον.

*... shouting, "Men of Israel, help! This is the man who teaches everyone everywhere against our people, our law, and this place. What's more, he also brought Greeks into the temple and **profanes** this holy place."*

Acts 25:11 εἰ μὲν οὖν ἀδικῶ καὶ ἄξιον θανάτου **πέπραχά** τι, οὐ παραιτοῦμαι τὸ ἀποθανεῖν· εἰ δὲ οὐδέν ἐστιν ὧν οὗτοι κατηγοροῦσίν μου, οὐδείς με δύναται αὐτοῖς χαρίσασθαι· Καίσαρα ἐπικαλοῦμαι.

*"If then I am doing wrong, or **am doing** anything deserving of death, I do not refuse to die, but if there is nothing to what these men accuse me of, no one can give me up to them. I appeal to Caesar!"*

1 Corinthians 7:15   εἰ δὲ ὁ ἄπιστος χωρίζεται, χωριζέσθω· οὐ δεδούλωται ὁ ἀδελφὸς ἢ ἡ ἀδελφὴ ἐν τοῖς τοιούτοις· ἐν δὲ εἰρήνῃ **κέκληκεν** ὑμᾶς ὁ θεός.

*But if the unbeliever leaves, let him leave. A brother or a sister is not bound in such cases. God **calls** you to peace.*

2 Timothy 4:7   τὸν καλὸν ἀγῶνα **ἠγώνισμαι**, τὸν δρόμον **τετέλεκα**, τὴν πίστιν **τετήρηκα**.

*I **am fighting** the good fight, I **am finishing** the race, I **am keeping** the faith.*

Pragmatics of Heightened Proximity

There is an extra step required in translating perfects. The spatial value of heightened proximity adds another level to the analysis of perfect tense-forms above *Aktionsart*. Once the *Aktionsart* of a particular perfect is established, the pragmatic expression of heightened proximity must be addressed. The semantic value of heightened proximity may be expressed pragmatically in one of two key ways: intensification or prominence. It is not always clear as to which pragmatic expression is most suitable in particular instances, but a basic rule of thumb is to see if intensification is possible or likely; if not, prominence is expressed rather than intensification.

Intensification

Because heightened proximity creates a super closeup view of an action, it may cause some actions to become intensified. This means that the transitive lexeme is "sharpened" beyond its normal usage.

The following examples demonstrate the manner in which a perfect may intensify a lexeme beyond its normal meaning: ἥγημαι, "be firmly convinced" (ἡγοῦμαι, "believe, think"), τεθαύμακα, "be surprised" (θαυμάζω, "wonder, marvel"), πεφόβημαι, "be terrified" (φοβοῦμαι, "be afraid"), σεσιώπηκα, "maintain complete silence" (σιωπῶ, "be silent").[2]

---

2. See Albert Rijksbaron, *The Syntax and Semantics of the Verb in Classical Greek: An Introduction* (Amsterdam: Gieben, 1984), 36.

Prominence

When intensification is not easily applied to a lexeme or is not deemed appropriate in the context, prominence is the pragmatic expression of heightened proximity. The concept of prominence is here taken to refer to the degree to which an element stands out from others in its environment. Thus, prominence is roughly synonymous with *stress*. Often such prominence is not easily expressed in English translation, though the use of italics should be considered as a legitimate technique for this purpose in some instances.

Nonindicative Usage (Perfect Tense-Form): Participle

The perfect participle semantically encodes imperfective aspect. It is its aspect that leads to the perfect participle's main pragmatic function in which it nearly always expresses action that is contemporaneous with its leading verb. The usage of the perfect participle, therefore, parallels that of the present participle.

While the spatial values of proximity and remoteness are generally not encoded in nonindicative verbs, the perfect participle encodes the spatial value of proximity, which distinguishes it from the present participle. It is not normally possible to reflect this difference in translation.

Luke 9:27 λέγω δὲ ὑμῖν ἀληθῶς, εἰσίν τινες τῶν αὐτοῦ **ἑστηκότων** οἳ οὐ μὴ γεύσωνται θανάτου ἕως ἂν ἴδωσιν τὴν βασιλείαν τοῦ θεοῦ.

*I tell you the truth: there are some **standing** here who will not taste death until they see the kingdom of God.*

John 1:51 καὶ λέγει αὐτῷ· ἀμὴν ἀμὴν λέγω ὑμῖν, ὄψεσθε τὸν οὐρανὸν **ἀνεῳγότα** καὶ τοὺς ἀγγέλους τοῦ θεοῦ ἀναβαίνοντας καὶ καταβαίνοντας ἐπὶ τὸν υἱὸν τοῦ ἀνθρώπου.

*Then he said, "I assure you: You will see heaven **opening** and the angels of God ascending and descending on the Son of Man."*

Romans 5:3 οὐ μόνον δέ, ἀλλὰ καὶ καυχώμεθα ἐν ταῖς θλίψεσιν, **εἰδότες** ὅτι ἡ θλῖψις ὑπομονὴν κατεργάζεται,

*And not only that, but we also rejoice in our afflictions, **knowing** that affliction produces endurance.*

Aktionsart Interactions (Pluperfect Tense-Form)

There are only a few ways in which the pluperfect tense-form functions pragmatically. Below are the most common and important *Aktionsart* descriptions of pluperfect usage along with explanations of how the *Aktionsart* values are arrived at. It will be noticed that the pluperfect is similar in usage to the imperfect tense-form. This is to be expected, given their sharing of imperfective aspect and remoteness.

The word "had" in translation of pluperfects comes from the traditional understanding of the pluperfect, in which the verb was understood as conveying an action antecedent to the past action of the main verb and consequences present at the time of that past action. While rendering the pluperfect will often require the word "had" in our translations, this should not be supplied by default. Context will determine whether "had" needs to be included in our translation. Pluperfects will normally refer either to the past, in which they stand parallel to imperfects, or to the *past-past*, in which they stand "behind" imperfects and need to be rendered with "had" in translation.

Stative

Pluperfect tense-forms often end up depicting a state. This is also a natural implicature of imperfective aspect. Imperfective aspect combines with a stative lexeme to create a stative *Aktionsart*, if this is not overturned by context. A stative lexeme is a word that describes a state of being rather than a process or transitive action. Sometimes the context can create a stative *Aktionsart* even if the lexeme is not in itself stative.

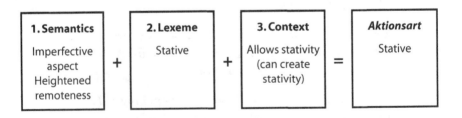

Luke 23:10 εἱστήκεισαν δὲ οἱ ἀρχιερεῖς καὶ οἱ γραμματεῖς εὐτόνως κατηγοροῦντες αὐτοῦ.

*The chief priests and the scribes **were standing by**, vehemently accusing him.*

John 2:9 ὡς δὲ ἐγεύσατο ὁ ἀρχιτρίκλινος τὸ ὕδωρ οἶνον γεγενημένον καὶ **οὐκ ἤδει** πόθεν ἐστίν, οἱ δὲ διάκονοι **ᾔδεισαν** οἱ ἠντληκότες τὸ ὕδωρ, φωνεῖ τὸν νυμφίον ὁ ἀρχιτρίκλινος.

When the chief servant tasted the water (after it had become wine), ***he did not know*** *where it came from—though the servants who had drawn the water* ***knew***, *the chief servant called the bridegroom.*

Luke 4:29 καὶ ἀναστάντες ἐξέβαλον αὐτὸν ἔξω τῆς πόλεως καὶ ἤγαγον αὐτὸν ἕως ὀφρύος τοῦ ὄρους ἐφ᾽ οὗ ἡ πόλις **ᾠκοδόμητο** αὐτῶν ὥστε κατακρημνίσαι αὐτόν.

They got up, drove him out of town, and brought him to the edge of the hill their town ***was built on***, *intending to hurl him over the cliff.*

Past-Past ("Had")

The pluperfect often depicts action that is past in the past—it refers to a time frame that stands behind an already past temporal context. This is a unique function of the pluperfect, which is suited to this because of its heightened remoteness; past-past temporal reference is doubly remote. This use of the pluperfect can involve any type of lexeme and arises from contextual factors. The word "had" is appropriate in translating past-past pluperfects.

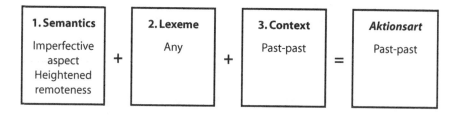

Mark 15:7 ἦν δὲ ὁ λεγόμενος Βαραββᾶς μετὰ τῶν στασιαστῶν δεδεμένος οἵτινες ἐν τῇ στάσει φόνον **πεποιήκεισαν**.

There was one named Barabbas, who was in prison with rebels who ***had committed*** *murder during the rebellion.*

Luke 22:13 ἀπελθόντες δὲ εὗρον καθὼς **εἰρήκει** αὐτοῖς καὶ ἡτοίμασαν τὸ πάσχα.

So they went and found it just as ***he had told*** *them, and they prepared the Passover.*

John 7:30 Ἐζήτουν οὖν αὐτὸν πιάσαι, καὶ οὐδεὶς ἐπέβαλεν ἐπ᾽ αὐτὸν τὴν χεῖρα, ὅτι **οὔπω ἐληλύθει** ἡ ὥρα αὐτοῦ.

*Then they tried to seize him. Yet no one laid a hand on him because his hour **had not yet come**.*

Exercises for Perfect and Pluperfect Tense-forms

For each passage, (1) write about the semantic meaning of the verb, (2) state the contribution of the lexeme, and (3) discuss the function of the verb in context. Once you have written your answers, summarize your findings in the boxes below each passage.

Example:

John 7:27 ἀλλὰ τοῦτον **οἴδαμεν** πόθεν ἐστίν· ὁ δὲ χριστὸς ὅταν ἔρχηται οὐδεὶς γινώσκει πόθεν ἐστίν.

*But **we know** where this man is from. When the Christ comes, nobody will know where he is from.*

1. Semantic meaning of the verb. The perfect indicative semantically encodes imperfective aspect and the spatial value of heightened proximity.
2. Contribution of the lexeme. The lexeme is stative
3. Function in context. The context allows stativity.

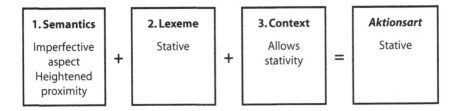

Romans 1:17 δικαιοσύνη γὰρ θεοῦ ἐν αὐτῷ ἀποκαλύπτεται ἐκ πίστεως εἰς πίστιν, καθὼς **γέγραπται**· ὁ δὲ δίκαιος ἐκ πίστεως ζήσεται.

*For in it God's righteousness is revealed from faith to faith, just as **it is written**: The righteous will live by faith.*

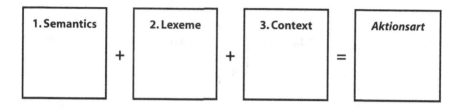

John 7:30 Ἐζήτουν οὖν αὐτὸν πιάσαι, καὶ οὐδεὶς ἐπέβαλεν ἐπ᾽ αὐτὸν τὴν χεῖρα, ὅτι **οὔπω ἐληλύθει** ἡ ὥρα αὐτοῦ.

*Then they tried to seize him. Yet no one laid a hand on him because his hour **had not yet come**.*

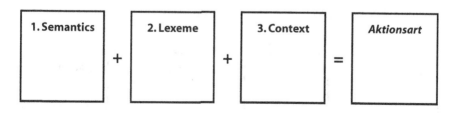

John 16:11 περὶ δὲ κρίσεως, ὅτι ὁ ἄρχων τοῦ κόσμου τούτου **κέκριται**.

*... and about judgment, because the ruler of this world **is being judged**.*

John 1:15 Ἰωάννης μαρτυρεῖ περὶ αὐτοῦ καὶ **κέκραγεν** λέγων· οὗτος ἦν ὃν εἶπον· ὁ ὀπίσω μου ἐρχόμενος ἔμπροσθέν μου γέγονεν, ὅτι πρῶτός μου ἦν.

*John testified concerning him and **exclaimed**, "This was the One of whom I said, 'The One coming after me has surpassed me, because he was before me.'"*

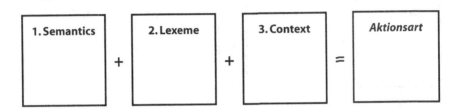

Romans 8:38 **πέπεισμαι** γὰρ ὅτι οὔτε θάνατος οὔτε ζωὴ οὔτε ἄγγελοι οὔτε ἀρχαὶ οὔτε ἐνεστῶτα οὔτε μέλλοντα οὔτε δυνάμεις …

*For **I am persuaded** that neither death nor life, nor angels nor rulers, nor things present, nor things to come, nor powers…*

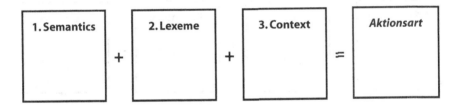

Matthew 7:25 καὶ κατέβη ἡ βροχὴ καὶ ἦλθον οἱ ποταμοὶ καὶ ἔπνευσαν οἱ ἄνεμοι καὶ προσέπεσαν τῇ οἰκίᾳ ἐκείνῃ, καὶ οὐκ ἔπεσεν, **τεθεμελίωτο** γὰρ ἐπὶ τὴν πέτραν.

*The rain fell, the rivers rose, and the winds blew and pounded that house. Yet it didn't collapse, because **it was founded** on the rock.*

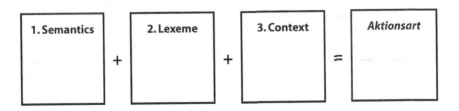

John 19:30 ὅτε οὖν ἔλαβεν τὸ ὄξος [ὁ] Ἰησοῦς εἶπεν· **τετέλεσται**, καὶ κλίνας τὴν κεφαλὴν παρέδωκεν τὸ πνεῦμα.

When Jesus had received the sour wine, he said, "It is finished!" Then after bowing his head, he gave up his spirit.

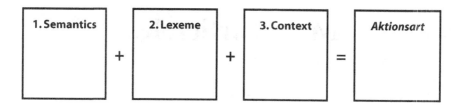

John 20:11 Μαρία δὲ **εἱστήκει** πρὸς τῷ μνημείῳ ἔξω κλαίουσα. ὡς οὖν ἔκλαιεν, παρέκυψεν εἰς τὸ μνημεῖον.

But Mary was standing outside facing the tomb, crying. As she was crying, she stooped to look into the tomb.

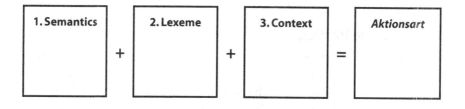

Chapter 10

More Participles

—∽∾∽—

While the basic operations of adverbial participles are discussed within previous chapters, it is worth discussing separately the topics of periphrastic participles, adjectival and substantival participles, and participles of attendant circumstance.

Periphrastic Participles

Periphrastic participles are participles that form a construction with a finite auxiliary verb that provides a net meaning. For most of these constructions, the net meaning of the construction corresponds to the meaning of a particular finite form. Periphrases in the New Testament involve only the present and perfect participles, which may be combined with present, imperfect, or future finite auxiliaries, normally of εἰμί, as the table below sets forth.[1]

The Forms of the Periphrastic Participle

Finite Verb (of εἰμί)	+ Participle	Finite Tense Equivalent
Present	+ Present Participle	Present
Imperfect	+ Present Participle	Imperfect
Future	+ Present Participle	Future
Present	+ Perfect Participle	Perfect
Imperfect	+ Perfect Participle	Pluperfect

---

1. The table is from Daniel B. Wallace, *Greek Grammar beyond the Basics: An Exegetical Syntax of the New Testament* (Grand Rapids: Zondervan, 1996), 648.

Following are examples of each type of periphrasis.

Present Periphrasis

John 1:41 εὑρίσκει οὗτος πρῶτον τὸν ἀδελφὸν τὸν ἴδιον
Σίμωνα καὶ λέγει αὐτῷ· εὑρήκαμεν τὸν Μεσσίαν, ὅ **ἐστιν**
μεθερμηνευόμενον χριστός.

He first found his own brother Simon and told him, "We have found the
*Messiah!" (which **is translated** "Anointed One").*

Imperfect Periphrasis

John 1:28 ταῦτα ἐν Βηθανίᾳ ἐγένετο πέραν τοῦ Ἰορδάνου, ὅπου
ἦν ὁ Ἰωάννης **βαπτίζων**.

*All this happened in Bethany across the Jordan, where John **was***
***baptizing**.*

Future Periphrasis

Luke 1:20 καὶ ἰδοὺ **ἔσῃ σιωπῶν** καὶ μὴ δυνάμενος λαλῆσαι ἄχρι
ἧς ἡμέρας γένηται ταῦτα.

*Now listen! **You will become silent** and unable to speak until the day*
these things take place.

Perfect Periphrasis

John 3:27 ἀπεκρίθη Ἰωάννης καὶ εἶπεν· οὐ δύναται ἄνθρωπος
λαμβάνειν οὐδὲ ἕν ἐὰν μὴ **ᾖ δεδομένον** αὐτῷ ἐκ τοῦ οὐρανοῦ.

*John responded, "No one can receive a single thing unless **it is given** to*
him from heaven."

Pluperfect Periphrasis

Matthew 9:36 Ἰδὼν δὲ τοὺς ὄχλους ἐσπλαγχνίσθη περὶ αὐτῶν,
ὅτι **ἦσαν ἐσκυλμένοι** καὶ **ἐρριμμένοι** ὡσεὶ πρόβατα μὴ ἔχοντα
ποιμένα.

*When he saw the crowds, he felt compassion for them, because **they***
***were weary** and **worn out**, like sheep without a shepherd.*

In terms of verbal aspect, participial periphrastic contructions convey the same aspectual and spatial semantic values that their finite equivalents convey, with one exception, which will be noted below. This is because the aspect of the periphrasis is determined by the participle, not by the auxiliary. Once an indicative verb begins to function as the auxiliary within a periphrastic construction, it becomes "aspectually vague" and therefore does not contribute aspect to the net outcome.[2]

As such, a review of the table above reveals that all periphrastic constructions are imperfective in aspect, since the present and perfect participles that form these constructions are imperfective in aspect. In four out of five cases, the imperfective aspect of the periphrasis matches the imperfective aspect of the finite equivalent. For example, the imperfect periphrasis consists of the imperfect auxiliary and the present participle, which results in a periphrasis that expresses imperfective aspect. This is the same aspectual value as the imperfect indicative tense-form.

The one exception is the future periphrasis. If the aspectual value of the periphrasis is determined by the participle and not the auxiliary, then the future periphrasis must be imperfective in aspect, since the present participle that helps to form the periphrasis is imperfective. This is not, therefore, the same as the aspectual value of the future indicative tense-form, which is perfective in aspect. While such issues are difficult to resolve with certainty, it is most likely that the future periphrasis does not simply replicate the future indicative; rather, it provides an imperfective option for the future. Consequently, there is aspectual choice for the future—the perfective option is provided by the future indicative, while the imperfective option is provided by the future periphrasis.

Once these factors are appreciated, we may treat periphrastic constructions the same way that we have learned to deal with their finite counterparts. The same principles of exegesis apply, as do the various relationships between aspect, lexeme, and *Aktionsart*.

Adjectival Participles

Adjectival participles are participles that function like adjectives. They modify a noun, just as a normal adjective would, though they retain a verbal nuance. Nearly all adjectival participles are present or perfect. This is the case for the simple reason that offering description is a natural function of imperfective aspect.

---

2. See Campbell, *Non-Indicative Verbs*, 33–34.

Luke 7:32 ὅμοιοί εἰσιν παιδίοις τοῖς ἐν ἀγορᾷ **καθημένοις** καὶ **προσφωνοῦσιν** ἀλλήλοις.

*They are like children **sitting** in the marketplace and **calling** to each other.*

John 4:11 λέγει αὐτῷ [ἡ γυνή]· κύριε, οὔτε ἄντλημα ἔχεις καὶ τὸ φρέαρ ἐστὶν βαθύ· πόθεν οὖν ἔχεις τὸ ὕδωρ **τὸ ζῶν**;

"Sir," said the woman, "You don't even have a bucket, and the well is deep. So where do you get this 'living water'?"

Romans 12:1 Παρακαλῶ οὖν ὑμᾶς, ἀδελφοί, διὰ τῶν οἰκτιρμῶν τοῦ θεοῦ παραστῆσαι τὰ σώματα ὑμῶν θυσίαν **ζῶσαν** ἁγίαν εὐάρεστον τῷ θεῷ, τὴν λογικὴν λατρείαν ὑμῶν.

*Therefore, brothers, by the mercies of God, I urge you to present your bodies as a **living** sacrifice, holy and pleasing to God; this is your spiritual worship.*

Occasionally, however, an adjectival participle may be aorist. In such cases, the aorist is used in order to describe some kind of antecedence that relates to the noun that the participle modifies. This is a standard function of perfective aspect.

Romans 12:3 Λέγω γὰρ διὰ τῆς χάριτος **τῆς δοθείσης** μοι παντὶ τῷ ὄντι ἐν ὑμῖν μὴ ὑπερφρονεῖν παρ᾽ ὃ δεῖ φρονεῖν ἀλλὰ φρονεῖν εἰς τὸ σωφρονεῖν.

*For by the grace **given** to me, I tell everyone among you not to think of himself more highly than he should think.*

Substantival Participles

A substantival participle is one that functions as a substantive — that is, as a noun. There are many examples of this usage of the participle.

Luke 1:50 καὶ τὸ ἔλεος αὐτοῦ εἰς γενεὰς καὶ γενεὰς **τοῖς φοβουμένοις** αὐτόν.

*His mercy is from generation to generation on **those who fear** him.*

John 5:11 ὁ δὲ ἀπεκρίθη αὐτοῖς· **ὁ ποιήσας** με ὑγιῆ ἐκεῖνός μοι εἶπεν· ἆρον τὸν κράβαττόν σου καὶ περιπάτει.

*He replied to them, "**The man who made** me well told me, 'Pick up your bedroll and walk.' "*

John 6:39 τοῦτο δέ ἐστιν τὸ θέλημα **τοῦ πέμψαντός** με.

*This is the will of **the one who sent** me.*

While several scholars minimize the importance of aspect within this usage of the participle, there is nevertheless good evidence that aspect is relevant, even though the participle functions as a noun.

The Present Substantival Participle

Imperfective aspect is a semantic feature of the present participle, and this feature continues to play a role in the present participle's use as a substantive. Though functioning as a noun, there is often a verbal nuance to the noun when it is conveyed through a substantivalized participle. When the present is used, the verbal nuance is normally contemporaneous in time frame, just as the adverbial participle often is. This is a pragmatic outworking of imperfective aspect.

Luke 7:14 καὶ προσελθὼν ἥψατο τῆς σοροῦ, **οἱ δὲ βαστάζοντες** ἔστησαν, καὶ εἶπεν· νεανίσκε, σοὶ λέγω, ἐγέρθητι.

*Then he came up and touched the open coffin, and **those bearing** the coffin stopped. And he said, "Young man, I tell you, get up!"*

John 3:36 **ὁ πιστεύων** εἰς τὸν υἱὸν ἔχει ζωὴν αἰώνιον· **ὁ δὲ ἀπειθῶν** τῷ υἱῷ οὐκ ὄψεται ζωήν, ἀλλ᾽ ἡ ὀργὴ τοῦ θεοῦ μένει ἐπ᾽ αὐτόν.

*The one who believes in the Son has eternal life, but **the one who refuses to believe** in the Son will not see life; instead, the wrath of God remains on him.*

Romans 1:32 οἵτινες τὸ δικαίωμα τοῦ θεοῦ ἐπιγνόντες ὅτι **οἱ τὰ** τοιαῦτα **πράσσοντες** ἄξιοι θανάτου εἰσίν, οὐ μόνον αὐτὰ ποιοῦσιν ἀλλὰ καὶ συνευδοκοῦσιν **τοῖς πράσσουσιν**.

*Although they know full well God's just sentence—that **those who practice** such things deserve to die—they not only do them, but even applaud **others who practice** them.*

Another pragmatic outworking of imperfective aspect in present substantival participles is the providing of some kind of description or state.

Luke 16:26 καὶ ἐν πᾶσι τούτοις μεταξὺ ἡμῶν καὶ ὑμῶν χάσμα μέγα ἐστήρικται, ὅπως **οἱ θέλοντες διαβῆναι** ἔνθεν πρὸς ὑμᾶς μὴ δύνωνται, μηδὲ ἐκεῖθεν πρὸς ἡμᾶς διαπερῶσιν.

Besides all this, a great chasm has been fixed between us and you, so that ***those who want to pass over*** *from here to you cannot; neither can those from there cross over to us.*

Luke 22:36 εἶπεν δὲ αὐτοῖς· ἀλλὰ νῦν **ὁ ἔχων** βαλλάντιον ἀράτω, ὁμοίως καὶ πήραν, καὶ **ὁ μὴ ἔχων** πωλησάτω τὸ ἱμάτιον αὐτοῦ καὶ ἀγορασάτω μάχαιραν.

Then he said to them, "But now, ***whoever has*** *a money-bag should take it, and also a traveling bag. And* ***whoever doesn't have*** *a sword should sell his robe and buy one."*

A third pragmatic outworking of imperfective aspect is present substantive participles within generic or proverbial statements.

Luke 6:30 **παντὶ αἰτοῦντί σε** δίδου, καὶ ἀπὸ **τοῦ αἴροντος** τὰ σὰ μὴ ἀπαίτει.

Give to ***everyone who asks from you****, and from* ***one who takes away*** *your things, don't ask for them back.*

Luke 11:23 Ὁ **μὴ ὢν** μετ᾽ ἐμοῦ κατ᾽ ἐμοῦ ἐστιν, καὶ **ὁ μὴ συνάγων** μετ᾽ ἐμοῦ σκορπίζει.

Anyone who is not *with me is against me, and* ***anyone who does not gather*** *with me scatters.*

John 12:45 καὶ **ὁ θεωρῶν** ἐμὲ θεωρεῖ τὸν πέμψαντά με.

And ***the one who sees*** *me sees him who sent me.*

The Aorist Substantival Participle

Perfective aspect is a semantic feature of the aorist participle, and this feature continues to play a role in the aorist participle's use as a substantive. Though functioning as a noun, there is often a verbal nuance to the noun when it is conveyed through a substantivalized participle. When the aorist is used, the verbal nuance is normally antecedent in time frame, just as the adverbial participle often is. This is a pragmatic outworking of perfective aspect.

Luke 7:10 Καὶ ὑποστρέψαντες εἰς τὸν οἶκον **οἱ πεμφθέντες** εὗρον τὸν δοῦλον ὑγιαίνοντα.

*When **those who had been sent** returned to the house, they found the slave in good health.*

John 5:30 Οὐ δύναμαι ἐγὼ ποιεῖν ἀπ' ἐμαυτοῦ οὐδέν· καθὼς ἀκούω κρίνω, καὶ ἡ κρίσις ἡ ἐμὴ δικαία ἐστίν, ὅτι οὐ ζητῶ τὸ θέλημα τὸ ἐμὸν ἀλλὰ τὸ θέλημα **τοῦ πέμψαντός** με.

*I am not able to do anything from myself; as I hear, I judge, and my judgment is righteous, because I do not seek my own will, but the will **of him who sent** me.*

Romans 6:7 ὁ γὰρ **ἀποθανὼν** δεδικαίωται ἀπὸ τῆς ἁμαρτίας.

*... since **a person who has died** is freed from sin's claims.*

The Perfect Substantival Participle

Imperfective aspect is a semantic feature of the perfect participle, and this feature continues to play a role in the perfect participle's use as a substantive. Though functioning as a noun, there is often a verbal nuance to the noun when it is conveyed through a substantivalized participle. When the perfect is used, the verbal nuance is normally contemporaneous in time frame, just as the adverbial participle often is. This is a pragmatic outworking of imperfective aspect, and it mirrors the primary usage of the present substantival participle, which is to be expected since the two forms share the same aspect.

Matthew 5:10 μακάριοι **οἱ δεδιωγμένοι** ἕνεκεν δικαιοσύνης, ὅτι αὐτῶν ἐστιν ἡ βασιλεία τῶν οὐρανῶν.

*Blessed are **those who are persecuted** for righteousness, because the kingdom of heaven is theirs.*

Luke 6:25 οὐαὶ ὑμῖν, **οἱ ἐμπεπλησμένοι** νῦν, ὅτι πεινάσετε. οὐαί, οἱ γελῶντες νῦν, ὅτι πενθήσετε καὶ κλαύσετε.

*Woe to you, **those being full** now, because you will be hungry. Woe to you who are laughing now, because you will mourn and weep.*

Luke 19:24 καὶ **τοῖς παρεστῶσιν** εἶπεν· ἄρατε ἀπ' αὐτοῦ τὴν μνᾶν καὶ δότε τῷ τὰς δέκα μνᾶς ἔχοντι.

*So he said **to those standing there**, "Take the mina from him and give it to the one who has ten minas."*

Sometimes, however, the perfect substantival participles will demonstrate a nuance of past temporal reference. This normally occurs with lexemes of propulsion and introducers of discourse. In other words, the same lexemes that form historical perfects (and historical presents, for that matter) are those that have a sense of antecedent temporal reference with perfect substantival participles.

Matthew 23:37 Ἰερουσαλὴμ Ἰερουσαλήμ, ἡ ἀποκτείνουσα τοὺς προφήτας καὶ λιθοβολοῦσα **τοὺς ἀπεσταλμένους** πρὸς αὐτήν.

*Jerusalem, Jerusalem! The city who kills the prophets and stones **those who were sent** to her.*

Luke 1:45 καὶ μακαρία ἡ πιστεύσασα ὅτι ἔσται τελείωσις **τοῖς λελαλημένοις** αὐτῇ παρὰ κυρίου.

*She who has believed is blessed because **what was spoken** to her by the Lord will be fulfilled!*

Luke 14:12 Ἔλεγεν δὲ καὶ **τῷ κεκληκότι αὐτόν·** ὅταν ποιῇς ἄριστον ἢ δεῖπνον, μὴ φώνει τοὺς φίλους σου μηδὲ τοὺς ἀδελφούς σου μηδὲ τοὺς συγγενεῖς σου μηδὲ γείτονας πλουσίους, μήποτε καὶ αὐτοὶ ἀντικαλέσωσίν σε καὶ γένηται ἀνταπόδομά σοι.

*He also said **to the one who had invited him,** "When you give a dinner or a banquet, don't invite your friends, your brothers, your relatives, or your rich neighbors, lest they invite you back, and you be repaid."*

Participles of Attendant Circumstance

According to Wallace, a participle of attendant circumstance communicates an action that is coordinate with its finite leading verb, and " 'piggybacks' on the mood of the main verb."[3] The participle, therefore, takes on the force of a finite verb and ceases, in some sense, to behave like a participle. Again according to Wallace, participles of attendant circumstance are identified by the following features: the tense-form of the participle is usually aorist; the tense-form of the main verb is usually aorist; the mood of the main verb is usually imperative or indicative; the participle will precede the main verb; they occur frequently in narrative. These features are observed in the following examples.

---

3. Wallace, *Grammar*, 640.

Matthew 2:8 καὶ πέμψας αὐτοὺς εἰς Βηθλέεμ εἶπεν· **πορευθέντες ἐξετάσατε** ἀκριβῶς περὶ τοῦ παιδίου· ἐπὰν δὲ εὕρητε, ἀπαγγείλατέ μοι, ὅπως κἀγὼ ἐλθὼν προσκυνήσω αὐτῷ.

*He sent them to Bethlehem and said, "*Go *and* search *carefully for the child. When you find him, report back to me so that I too may go and worship him."*

Matthew 28:7 καὶ ταχὺ **πορευθεῖσαι εἴπατε** τοῖς μαθηταῖς αὐτοῦ ὅτι ἠγέρθη ἀπὸ τῶν νεκρῶν, καὶ ἰδοὺ προάγει ὑμᾶς εἰς τὴν Γαλιλαίαν, ἐκεῖ αὐτὸν ὄψεσθε· ἰδοὺ εἶπον ὑμῖν.

Then go *quickly and* tell *his disciples, "He has been raised from the dead. In fact, he is going ahead of you to Galilee; you will see him there." Listen, I have told you.*

Luke 1:19 καὶ **ἀποκριθεὶς** ὁ ἄγγελος **εἶπεν** αὐτῷ· ἐγώ εἰμι Γαβριὴλ ὁ παρεστηκὼς ἐνώπιον τοῦ θεοῦ καὶ ἀπεστάλην λαλῆσαι πρὸς σὲ καὶ εὐαγγελίσασθαί σοι ταῦτα.

The angel answered *him, "I am Gabriel, who stands in the presence of God, and I was sent to speak to you and tell you this good news."*

In terms of aspect, the significance of participles of attendant circumstance is that they are contemporaneous with the leading verb, even though they are aorist participles. In such cases, the perfective aspect of the aorist participle functions to coordinate with the perfective aspect of its aorist leading verb. This is the pragmatic function of perfective aspect here rather than the more usual expression of antecedent temporal reference.

In terms of exegetical significance, recognition of participles of attendant circumstance is important. As the first two examples above demonstrate, participles of attendant circumstance may take on the meaning of the imperative mood rather than expressing some kind of prior action before a command is to be carried out. A classic example is found in Matthew 28:19.

Matthew 28:19 **πορευθέντες** οὖν **μαθητεύσατε** πάντα τὰ ἔθνη, βαπτίζοντες αὐτοὺς εἰς τὸ ὄνομα τοῦ πατρὸς καὶ τοῦ υἱοῦ καὶ τοῦ ἁγίου πνεύματος.

Go, therefore, and make disciples *of all nations, baptizing them in the name of the Father and of the Son and of the Holy Spirit.*

It would be a mistake to render this aorist participle "as you go," communicating an action that frames the context in which the command "make disciples" is to take place. Instead, as a participle of attendant circumstance, the aorist takes on the full force of the imperative with which it is coordinate. The command is to go and make disciples.

Exercises for the Participle

For each participle encountered, work out whether it is periphrastic, adjectival, substantival, or a participle of attendant circumstance. Then identify the aspect of the participle and describe what it is doing in the context.

Example:

John 16:5 νῦν δὲ ὑπάγω πρὸς τὸν **πέμψαντά** με, καὶ οὐδεὶς ἐξ ὑμῶν ἐρωτᾷ με· ποῦ ὑπάγεις;

But now I am going away to the one who sent me, and not one of you asks me, "Where are you going?"

1. Periphrastic, adjectival, substantival, or attendant circumstance? This participle is substantival.
2. What is the aspectual value? This aorist participle is perfective in aspect.
3. What is the participle doing in the context? This substantival participle conveys a nuance of past temporal reference.

John 5:2 Ἔστιν δὲ ἐν τοῖς Ἱεροσολύμοις ἐπὶ τῇ προβατικῇ κολυμβήθρα ἡ **ἐπιλεγομένη** Ἑβραϊστὶ Βηθζαθὰ πέντε στοὰς ἔχουσα.

By the Sheep Gate in Jerusalem there is a pool, called Bethesda in Hebrew, which has five colonnades.

Luke 16:6 ὁ δὲ εἶπεν· ἑκατὸν βάτους ἐλαίου. ὁ δὲ εἶπεν αὐτῷ· δέξαι σου τὰ γράμματα καὶ **καθίσας** ταχέως γράψον πεντήκοντα.

"A hundred measures of oil," he said. "Take your invoice," he told him, "sit down quickly, and write fifty."

John 13:23 ἦν **ἀνακείμενος** εἷς ἐκ τῶν μαθητῶν αὐτοῦ ἐν τῷ κόλπῳ τοῦ Ἰησοῦ, ὃν ἠγάπα ὁ Ἰησοῦς.

One of his disciples, the one Jesus loved, was reclining close beside Jesus.

Romans 7:14   Οἴδαμεν γὰρ ὅτι ὁ νόμος πνευματικός ἐστιν, ἐγὼ δὲ σάρκινός εἰμι **πεπραμένος** ὑπὸ τὴν ἁμαρτίαν.

*For we know that the law is spiritual; but I am made out of flesh, **sold** into sin's power.*

Acts 5:5   ἀκούων δὲ ὁ Ἀνανίας τοὺς λόγους τούτους **πεσὼν** ἐξέψυξεν, καὶ ἐγένετο φόβος μέγας ἐπὶ πάντας τοὺς ἀκούοντας.

*When he heard these words, Ananias **dropped** dead, and a great fear came on all who heard.*

John 3:24   οὔπω γὰρ ἦν **βεβλημένος** εἰς τὴν φυλακὴν ὁ Ἰωάννης.

*... since John had not yet **been thrown** into prison.*

Mark 14:69   καὶ ἡ παιδίσκη ἰδοῦσα αὐτὸν ἤρξατο πάλιν λέγειν τοῖς **παρεστῶσιν** ὅτι οὗτος ἐξ αὐτῶν ἐστιν.

*When the servant saw him again she began to tell those **standing** nearby, "This man is one of them!"*

A Concluding Postscript: Space and Time

—⁓—

Some readers may find the connection between spatial and temporal concepts confusing, and this postscript is intended to further clarify this relationship without making the main body of the book more complicated than it need be. It is claimed in this book that Greek verbs semantically encode aspect along with the spatial value of remoteness or proximity (with the exception of the future tense-form, which encodes aspect and future temporal reference). The difference between this description of the semantics of verbs and that of traditional analyses is that semantic temporal reference ("tense") has been replaced by semantic spatial categories. In other words, while traditional analyses might regard verbs as encoding aspect and tense, here verbs are regarded as encoding aspect and remoteness or aspect and proximity.

It is also claimed that these spatial values of remoteness and proximity, which are semantic, normally express temporal reference on the pragmatic level. This means that remoteness, for example, will most often be pragmatically expressed as temporal remoteness—the action is past-referring. The spatial value of proximity will most often express temporal proximity—present time. The question that might be asked is: how does a spatial value transmute into a temporal one?

Spatial Terms Are Metaphorical

First, it should be understood that the terms "remoteness" and "proximity" are best regarded as metaphors. When an aorist is used, it does not mean that the action occurred far away in a geographical sense, just because it because it encodes the spatial value of remoteness. For example, if I were to describe an action that occurred on my street, I am not forced to employ a proximate tense-form simply because it happened close to me physically. By the same token, if the action occurred in Cuba, I would not be forced to use a remote tense-form simply because Cuba is on the other side of the planet from Australia. To conclude that an action must have occurred at a physical distance because remoteness is encoded by the verb is to take remoteness literally—or concretely—rather than metaphorically.

It should be remembered that aspect itself is a subjective depiction of an action, event, or state. Remoteness and proximity are also employed as part of such a depiction. An action may be *portrayed* as remote without physically being distant. An action may be portrayed as proximate without physically being near.

Spatial and Temporal Remoteness

Second, remoteness and proximity are, by definition, spatial terms. The primary meaning of remoteness has to do with being *far away, distant*, and *removed*. It is by extension of this spatial meaning that remoteness can be applied to temporal expressions in English. For example, to speak of *the remote past* is to speak of time that is far away, distant, or removed. The spatial idea of remoteness has been applied to time. The "time" is remote. This can only really be a metaphorical expression, since time does not actually have a spatial dimension; it cannot actually be distant or near, because time is temporal, not spatial.

But therein lies the point. In English, we use spatial terms to describe time, and most of the time we do it without even noticing. *The remote past* is just one example. *The near future* is another. *Near* is no more a temporal term than *remote*, and yet we use the term in order to express temporal ideas. Again, the use is metaphorical. The future cannot spatially be near or far; the future cannot be on my street, or in Cuba. Time just doesn't occupy space, but this doesn't stop us speaking of it as though it does.

There are several other words in English that are actually spatial descriptors, but which are regularly employed for statements about time. Consider the word *next*. Is it temporal or spatial? You might answer, "Actually *next* has to do with order, which is neither temporal nor spatial." If that's what you're thinking, I'd say you're right and wrong. You're right that *next* has to do with order, but you're wrong that it's neither temporal nor spatial. It is, in fact, spatial. Order itself is primarily a spatial concept. It has to do with one thing after another—like children standing in line.

If they stand in alphabetical order, they arrange themselves spatially. Each child takes a position in relation to each other child's position. Things *in order* denotes things in a particular spatial arrangement in relation to one another. The word *next*, then, is actually a spatial term: the next street, the next house, the next room.

It is only by extension that this spatial word is applied to temporal situations. When we say *next week*, we are, of course, speaking about time—*week* tells us that. The contribution of *next* is to indicate that the week in question is following the current week. We think of it as *next* in the same way that we think of the *next house* as next. It is adjacent. And so we see that this spatial word is used to describe time, and that is normal in modern English usage.

There are several other examples of this phenomenon. The following words are, I would argue, primarily spatial in meaning, yet may be applied to time in normal English usage: *following* (as in *the following day*), *short* (as in *a short time*), *long* (as in *a long time*), *away* (as in *three weeks away*), *close* (as in *the day is getting close*), *distant* (as in *the distant past*), *far* (as in *far off into the future*).

The point of all this is simply to say that there is a much closer connection between time and space, even within our own language, than we may realize. We frequently use spatial descriptions in our communication of time, and we are capable of conceiving time through spatial metaphors.

Space and Time in History

The connection between space and time is arguably part of any language. Languages that encode time through their verbal system (i.e., languages that have tenses) did not necessarily always do this. All languages change over time, and one of the major changes that can be observed in the history of a number of languages is that the verbal system tends to begin as a spatial system and later develops into a temporal one. In other words, the idea that verbs should primarily convey actions in a spatial, rather than temporal, way is not unusual in the history of language, and several languages began in such a way.

The development from spatial to temporal systems within languages matches observations that anthropologists have made about cultures in general. They observe that in the development of many cultures, there is a development from a spatial way of thinking to a temporal way of thinking. Tony Swain, of the University of Sydney, has observed this in relation to certain tribes of Aboriginal Australians. These tribes apparently did not conceive of time at all in the way they thought; they thought about the world in a primarily spatial manner. It was not until they encountered Europeans that these tribes began to think in temporal categories.[1]

Such is the case with Greek. Most scholars would agree that the verbal system of Greek was originally spatial, back in its earliest stages of development. And, of course, the Greek verbal system is now temporal—Modern Greek has tenses. The question, however, is this: When did the verbal system cease to be primarily spatial and develop its temporal characteristics? While most scholars see the verbal system as consisting of tenses as early as Homeric Greek, and certainly by the time of Attic Greek, I have argued that the verbal system is still primarily spatial at this time and indeed continues to be so through the Koine period.

There is, nevertheless, evidence that the development from spatial to temporal meaning is taking place by this time. For example, the existence of the future tense-form, which is a real tense, is the first verb form that has a consistent temporal reference. It is a genuine tense, with its core meaning concerned with the expression of time. The existence of a real tense alongside other verb forms that are not regarded as tenses at the semantic level does not constitute a problem for my analysis, nor is it inconsistent. It is no accident that the only real tense within the indicative mood is also the last of the ancient tense-forms to develop. It is thus evidence that the shift from spatial to temporal encoding is taking place in the diachronic development of the language. Eventually, the entire indicative system will consist of tenses, and the future tense is the first exponent of this new situation.

Conclusion

Most students grappling with the relationship between space and time in language will want to know how to think about Greek verbs if they are to think of them spatially rather than temporally. The way forward, I think, is to realize that space and time often go together in English, and Greek is no different, though perhaps the ordering of the relationship is reversed.

In English, an event that occurred a long time ago will often be interpreted temporally first (it was a long time ago), but it will also have spatial implications for the way we think about the event. It might feel distant. Thus in English usage, the verb primarily conveys time, and yet has spatial implications for our thinking.

---

1. Tony Swain, *A Place for Strangers: Towards a History of Australian Aboriginal Being* (Cambridge: Cambridge University Press, 1993), 14–44.

Greek is like this, but in reverse. An event that is distant will be interpreted first spatially (it's the remote past), but will also have temporal implications for the way the language user thinks about the event (it happened a long time ago). In Greek, the verb primarily conveys remoteness or proximity and yet has temporal implications for our thinking.

Verbal Glossary

—✺—

Aktionsart
A category of pragmatics that describes actional characteristics, such as iterative, punctiliar, ingressive, etc. *Aktionsart* describes the combination of aspect with lexeme and context. It is therefore cancelable.

Aspect
The view of an action presented by the author. Internal or external viewpoints are the usual aspects. Not to be confused with *Aktionsart*. Aspect is semantic and therefore uncancelable.

Cancelability
A value is cancelable if it is not expressed with *every* use of a particular form. A value is uncancelable if it is expressed with every use of a particular form. Verbal semantic values are uncancelable, while pragmatic values are cancelable.

Conative *Aktionsart*
A verb depicts an attempted (but not accomplished) action. This may occur with imperfect tense-forms and any type of lexeme. Context indicates that the action was unsuccessfully attempted.

Deictic markers
Factors within text that indicate time, person, location, etc. Temporal deixis is most relevant here and encompasses words such as "now," "later," "before," "yesterday," etc. Narrative will often express temporal deixis without explicit markers since it is usually assumed to be referring to the past.

Gnomic *Aktionsart*

A verb depicts a timeless and universal action. This may occur with either aspect and any type of lexeme. Context alone determines whether or not an action is gnomic.

Historical perfect

A perfect tense-form that refers to the past.

Historical present

A present tense-form that refers to the past.

Imperfective aspect

The internal aspect/viewpoint. This depicts an action from the inside *as though* unfolding, without reference to the beginning or end of the action. It does not imply progression or incompleteness, though these *Aktionsarten* are naturally expressed with imperfective aspect in combination with other factors. The present, imperfect, perfect, and pluperfect tense-forms are imperfective in aspect.

Ingressive *Aktionsart*

A verb depicts the beginning, and subsequent progression, of an action. This may occur with imperfective aspect and any nonpunctiliar/nonstative lexeme, when the context indicates a shift or new direction. Alternatively, this may occur with perfective aspect and a stative lexeme.

Intransitive lexeme

A lexeme that does not perform an action upon an object. It may actually take an object, but strictly speaking the action is not *done to* the object. The action may be done with reference to someone or something.

Iterative *Aktionsart*

A verb depicts a repeated action. This may occur when imperfective aspect combines with a punctiliar lexeme. Alternatively, the context may create an iterative action even if the lexeme is not punctiliar.

Lexeme

A particular word, such as *run, write, see, fly,* etc.

Perfective aspect

The external aspect/viewpoint. This depicts an action as undefined, in summary, and somewhat remote. It does not imply completion or punctiliarity, though these *Aktionsarten* are naturally expressed with perfective aspect in combination with other factors. The aorist and future are perfective in aspect.

Pragmatics
The cancelable outcome of all textual/lexical/deictic factors in combination. What a verb ends up "doing" in the context.

Progressive *Aktionsart*
A verb depicts a process or action in progress. This may occur when imperfective aspect combines with any lexeme that is not punctiliar or stative and when the context allows progression.

Proximity
The spatial quality of nearness. Used as a spatial replacement for present tense. Spatial proximity may be expressed pragmatically through present temporal reference, or through logical intimacy (such as intensity or prominence).

Punctiliar *Aktionsart*
A verb depicts a punctiliar action. This may occur with perfective aspect and a punctiliar lexeme.

Punctiliar lexeme
A type of transitive lexeme that is instantaneous and once-occurring. While a punctiliar action may be repeated, it cannot be performed with any duration.

Remoteness
The spatial quality of distance. Used as a spatial replacement for past tense. Spatial remoteness may be expressed pragmatically through past temporal reference or through logical obliqueness (such as within negative conditions).

Semantics
The uncancelable core value/s of a verb form. With respect to verbs (verbal semantics, grammatical semantics), the semantic values are aspect and remoteness or proximity (or tense).

Stative *Aktionsart*
A verb depicts a state. This may occur when imperfective aspect combines with a stative lexeme. Sometimes the context can create a stative *Aktionsart* even if the lexeme is not itself stative.

Stative aspect

Refers either to the state of the subject (McKay) or of "the situation" (Porter). The latter is roughly equivalent to the "present consequence" of the traditional rendering of the perfect as past action with present consequence. It does not, in my view, accommodate transitive verbs very well. Under my analysis, stativity is properly understood as an *Aktionsart* category (as it is in general linguistics) rather than aspectual.

Stative lexeme

A type of intransitive lexeme that conveys a state of being.

Summary *Aktionsart*

A verb depicts a process or action in summary. This may occur with perfective aspect and any type of lexeme that is not punctiliar or stative.

Systemic linguistics

A school within functional linguistics, foundational especially to Porter's analysis. This conceives language use as a series of choices made in opposition to other possible choices. A language, therefore, is a network of oppositions.

Tense

Cancelable temporal reference. Tense has been mistakenly assumed by some to be semantic alongside aspect, but it is better regarded as a pragmatic outcome of various factors in context. In fact, on this definition one might say that tense does not exist; there is only temporal reference (except for the future, which is a real tense).

Transitive lexeme

A lexeme that performs an action upon an object.

Answers to Exercises

—◦∿◦—

Present and Imperfect Tense-Forms

For each passage, (1) write about the semantic meaning of the verb, (2) state the contribution of the lexeme, and (3) discuss the function of the verb in context. Once you have written your answers, summarize your findings in the boxes below each passage.

Example:

Luke 8:45 (x2) καὶ εἶπεν ὁ Ἰησοῦς· τίς ὁ ἁψάμενός μου; ἀρνουμένων δὲ πάντων εἶπεν ὁ Πέτρος· ἐπιστάτα, οἱ ὄχλοι **συνέχουσίν** σε καὶ **ἀποθλίβουσιν**.

*"Who touched Me?" Jesus asked. When they all denied it, Peter said, "Master, the crowds **are hemming** you in and **pressing against** you."*

1. Semantic meaning of the verb. The present indicative semantically encodes imperfective aspect and the spatial value of proximity.

2. Contribution of the lexeme. The lexemes are transitive (perform an action upon an object). They are not punctiliar or stative.

3. Function in context. The context makes it clear that these actions are taking place continuously at the time of speech. Thus, these verbs are conveying progressive action.

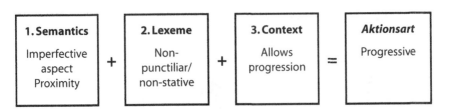

1. Semantics		2. Lexeme		3. Context		Aktionsart
Imperfective aspect Proximity	**+**	Non-punctiliar/ non-stative	**+**	Allows progression	**=**	Progressive

John 7:42 οὐχ ἡ γραφὴ εἶπεν ὅτι ἐκ τοῦ σπέρματος Δαυὶδ καὶ ἀπὸ Βηθλέεμ τῆς κώμης ὅπου ἦν Δαυὶδ **ἔρχεται** ὁ χριστός;

*Doesn't the Scripture say that the Christ **comes** from David's offspring and from the town of Bethlehem, where David once lived?*

1. Semantic meaning of the verb. The present indicative semantically encodes imperfective aspect and the spatial value of proximity.

2. Contribution of the lexeme. The lexeme is intransitive (does not take an object, but is not stative). This is also a verb of propulsion.

3. Function in context. The context makes it clear that a general statement about reality is being made and is therefore gnomic. Jesus is asserting the general statement that the Messiah comes from David's offspring.

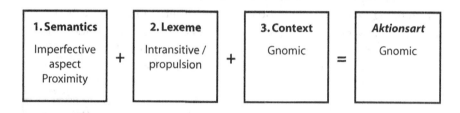

John 5:16 καὶ διὰ τοῦτο **ἐδίωκον** οἱ Ἰουδαῖοι τὸν Ἰησοῦν, ὅτι ταῦτα ἐποίει ἐν σαββάτῳ.

*Therefore, the Jews **began persecuting** Jesus because he was doing these things on the Sabbath.*

1. Semantic meaning of the verb. The imperfect indicative semantically encodes imperfective aspect and the spatial value of remoteness.

2. Contribution of the lexeme. The lexeme is transitive (takes an object), but not punctiliar.

3. Function in context. The context makes it clear that action has just begun, and as such the action is ingressive.

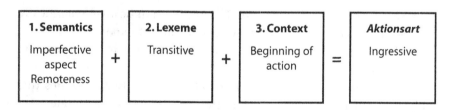

Romans 1:18 Ἀποκαλύπτεται γὰρ ὀργὴ θεοῦ ἀπ᾿ οὐρανοῦ ἐπὶ πᾶσαν ἀσέβειαν καὶ ἀδικίαν ἀνθρώπων τῶν τὴν ἀλήθειαν ἐν ἀδικίᾳ κατεχόντων,

*For God's wrath **is revealed** from heaven against all godlessness and unrighteousness of people who by their unrighteousness suppress the truth.*

1. Semantic meaning of the verb. The present indicative semantically encodes imperfective aspect and the spatial value of proximity.

2. Contribution of the lexeme. The lexeme is transitive. It is not punctiliar or stative.

3. Function in context. The context does not make it clear whether the action is progressive or stative. On the one hand, it may refer to God's wrath being revealed continuously; on the other, it may refer to a state of affairs (God's wrath has been revealed and is now evident). Wider context is needed to decide which option is best (i.e., theological context). An iterative reading is unlikely, since the lexeme is not punctiliar.

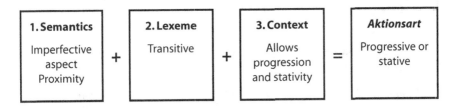

Romans 8:3 Τὸ γὰρ ἀδύνατον τοῦ νόμου ἐν ᾧ **ἠσθένει** διὰ τῆς σαρκός, ὁ θεὸς τὸν ἑαυτοῦ υἱὸν πέμψας ἐν ὁμοιώματι σαρκὸς ἁμαρτίας καὶ περὶ ἁμαρτίας κατέκρινεν τὴν ἁμαρτίαν ἐν τῇ σαρκί,

*What the law could not do since **it was limited** by the flesh, God did. He condemned sin in the flesh by sending his own Son in flesh like ours under sin's domain, and as a sin offering.*

1. Semantic meaning of the verb. The imperfect indicative semantically encodes imperfective aspect and the spatial value of remoteness.

2. Contribution of the lexeme. The lexeme is stative, in that it refers to being in a state of weakness.

3. Function in context. The context allows stativity, but locates this within a past temporal context. Thus, the verb conveys a (past) state.

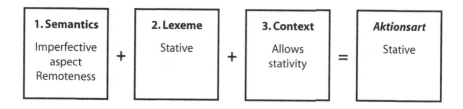

John 15:27 (x2) καὶ ὑμεῖς δὲ **μαρτυρεῖτε**, ὅτι ἀπ᾽ ἀρχῆς μετ᾽ ἐμοῦ **ἐστε**.

*You also **will testify**, because you **have been** with me from the beginning.*

1. Semantic meaning of the verb. The present indicative semantically encodes imperfective aspect and the spatial value of proximity.

2. Contribution of the lexeme. The first lexeme is intransitive (does not take an object, but is not stative); the second is stative.

3. Function in context. The context makes it clear that the first verb is progressive in nature and future in temporal reference. It is clear that the second verb refers to a state that began in the past ("from the beginning") and implies that the state exists at the time of speaking.

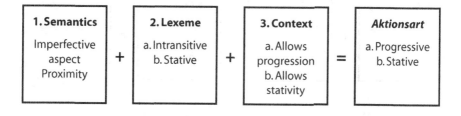

Romans 6:8 εἰ δὲ ἀπεθάνομεν σὺν Χριστῷ, **πιστεύομεν** ὅτι καὶ συζήσομεν αὐτῷ,

*Now if we died with Christ, **we believe** that we will also live with Him.*

1. Semantic meaning of the verb. The present indicative semantically encodes imperfective aspect and the spatial value of proximity.

2. Contribution of the lexeme. The lexeme is stative.

3. Function in context. The context allows stativity.

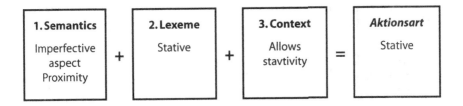

1. Semantics		2. Lexeme		3. Context		Aktionsart
Imperfective aspect Proximity	+	Stative	+	Allows stavtivity	=	Stative

John 3:22 Μετὰ ταῦτα ἦλθεν ὁ Ἰησοῦς καὶ οἱ μαθηταὶ αὐτοῦ εἰς τὴν Ἰουδαίαν γῆν καὶ ἐκεῖ διέτριβεν μετ' αὐτῶν καὶ **ἐβάπτιζεν**.

*After this, Jesus and his disciples went to the Judean countryside, where he spent time with them and **was baptizing**.*

1. Semantic meaning of the verb. The imperfect indicative semantically encodes imperfective aspect and the spatial value of remoteness.

2. Contribution of the lexeme. The lexeme is punctiliar, in that a baptism (lit., "to dip") is an instantaneous action.

3. Function in context. The context implies that this action was repeated and is therefore iterative.

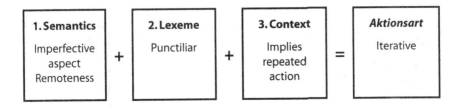

1. Semantics		2. Lexeme		3. Context		Aktionsart
Imperfective aspect Remoteness	+	Punctiliar	+	Implies repeated action	=	Iterative

Romans 8:13 (x3) εἰ γὰρ κατὰ σάρκα **ζῆτε, μέλλετε** ἀπο-θνῄ ΄σκειν· εἰ δὲ πνεύματι τὰς πράξεις τοῦ σώματος **θανατοῦτε**, ζήσεσθε.

For if **you live** according to the flesh, **you are going** to die. But if by the Spirit **you put to death** the deeds of the body, you will live.

1. Semantic meaning of the verb. The present indicative semantically encodes imperfective aspect and the spatial value of proximity.

2. Contribution of the lexeme. The first lexeme is stative; the second is an auxiliary to an infinitive (and is kind of stative); the third is transitive.

3. Function in context. The context allows the first and second verbs to be stative; the third is most likely progressive.

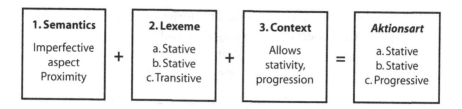

Aorist and Future Tense-Forms

For each passage, (1) write about the semantic meaning of the verb, (2) state the contribution of the lexeme, and (3) discuss the function of the verb in context. Once you have written your answers, summarize your findings in the boxes below each passage.

Example:

John 19:34 ἀλλ᾽ εἷς τῶν στρατιωτῶν λόγχῃ αὐτοῦ τὴν πλευρὰν **ἔνυξεν**, καὶ ἐξῆλθεν εὐθὺς αἷμα καὶ ὕδωρ.

*But one of the soldiers **pierced** his side with a spear, and at once blood and water came out.*

1. Semantic meaning of the verb. The aorist indicative semantically encodes perfective aspect and the spatial value of remoteness.
2. Contribution of the lexeme. The lexeme is punctiliar; it is an instantaneous action.
3. Function in context. The context allows punctiliarity.

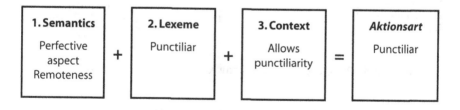

John 7:32 (x2) **ἤκουσαν** οἱ Φαρισαῖοι τοῦ ὄχλου γογγύζοντος περὶ αὐτοῦ ταῦτα, καὶ **ἀπέστειλαν** οἱ ἀρχιερεῖς καὶ οἱ Φαρισαῖοι ὑπηρέτας ἵνα πιάσωσιν αὐτόν.

*The Pharisees **heard** the crowd muttering these things about him, so the chief priests and the Pharisees **sent** temple police to arrest him.*

1. Semantic meaning of the verb. The aorist indicative semantically encodes perfective aspect and the spatial value of remoteness.

2. Contribution of the lexeme. Neither lexeme is punctiliar or stative.

3. Function in context. The context allows summary.

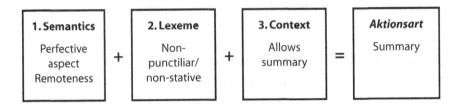

Romans 6:14 ἁμαρτία γὰρ ὑμῶν **οὐ κυριεύσει·** οὐ γάρ ἐστε ὑπὸ νόμον ἀλλὰ ὑπὸ χάριν.

*For sin **will not rule** over you, because you are not under law but under grace.*

1. Semantic meaning of the verb. The future indicative semantically encodes perfective aspect and future temporal reference.

2. Contribution of the lexeme. The lexeme is not punctiliar or stative.

3. Function in context. The context allows summary.

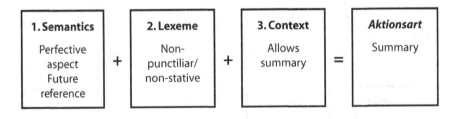

Romans 3:23 πάντες γὰρ **ἥμαρτον** καὶ ὑστεροῦνται τῆς δόξης τοῦ θεοῦ.

*For all **have sinned** and fall short of the glory of God.*

1. Semantic meaning of the verb. The aorist indicative semantically encodes perfective aspect and the spatial value of remoteness.

2. Contribution of the lexeme. The lexeme is not punctiliar or stative.

3. Function in context. The context allows summary. Could perhaps provide a gnomic context: "For all sin ..." but this is tentative at best.

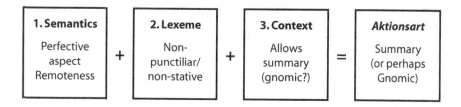

John 1:10 ἐν τῷ κόσμῳ ἦν, καὶ ὁ κόσμος δι᾽ αὐτοῦ ἐγένετο, καὶ ὁ κόσμος αὐτὸν **οὐκ ἔγνω**.

*He was in the world, and the world was created through him, yet the world **did not recognize** him.*

1. Semantic meaning of the verb. The aorist indicative semantically encodes perfective aspect and the spatial value of remoteness.

2. Contribution of the lexeme. The lexeme is stative.

3. Function in context. The context allows the entrance into a state.

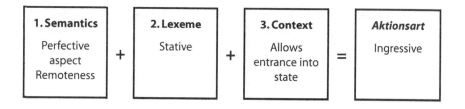

Mark 14:27 καὶ λέγει αὐτοῖς ὁ Ἰησοῦς ὅτι πάντες σκανδαλισθήσεσθε, ὅτι γέγραπται· **πατάξω** τὸν ποιμένα, καὶ τὰ πρόβατα διασκορπισθήσονται.

*Then Jesus said to them, "All of you will run away, because it is written: 'I **will strike** the shepherd, and the sheep will be scattered.' "*

1. Semantic meaning of the verb. The future indicative semantically encodes perfective aspect and future temporal reference.

2. Contribution of the lexeme. The lexeme is punctiliar; it is an instantaneous action.

3. Function in context. The context allows punctiliarity.

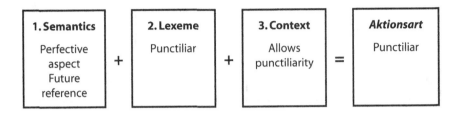

John 7:26 καὶ ἴδε παρρησίᾳ λαλεῖ καὶ οὐδὲν αὐτῷ λέγουσιν. μήποτε ἀληθῶς **ἔγνωσαν** οἱ ἄρχοντες ὅτι οὗτός ἐστιν ὁ χριστός;

*Yet, look! He's speaking publicly and they're saying nothing to him. Can it be true that the authorities **know** he is the Christ?*

1. Semantic meaning of the verb. The aorist indicative semantically encodes perfective aspect and the spatial value of remoteness.

2. Contribution of the lexeme. The lexeme is stative.

3. Function in context. The context allows entrance into a state.

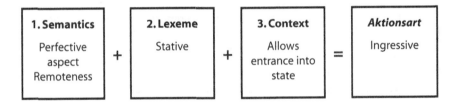

Romans 8:11 εἰ δὲ τὸ πνεῦμα τοῦ ἐγείραντος τὸν Ἰησοῦν ἐκ νεκρῶν οἰκεῖ ἐν ὑμῖν, ὁ ἐγείρας Χριστὸν ἐκ νεκρῶν **ζῳοποιήσει** καὶ τὰ θνητὰ σώματα ὑμῶν διὰ τοῦ ἐνοικοῦντος αὐτοῦ πνεύματος ἐν ὑμῖν.

*And if the Spirit of him who raised Jesus from the dead lives in you, then he who raised Christ from the dead **will also bring** your mortal bodies **to life** through his Spirit who lives in you.*

1. Semantic meaning of the verb. The future indicative semantically encodes perfective aspect and future temporal reference.

2. Contribution of the lexeme. The lexeme is not punctiliar or stative. It does, however, imply ingressive action, since it means "to make alive," which refers to the entrance into a state of being alive.

3. Function in context. The context allows entrance into a state.

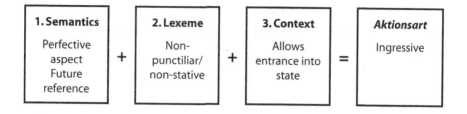

Romans 8:30 οὓς δὲ **προώρισεν**, τούτους καὶ **ἐκάλεσεν·** καὶ οὓς **ἐκάλεσεν**, τούτους καὶ **ἐδικαίωσεν·** οὓς δὲ **ἐδικαίωσεν**, τούτους καὶ **ἐδόξασεν**.

And those he predestines, he also calls; and those he calls, he also justifies; and those he justifies, he also glorifies.

1. Semantic meaning of the verb. The aorist indicative semantically encodes perfective aspect and the spatial value of remoteness.

2. Contribution of the lexeme. The lexemes are not punctiliar or stative.

3. Function in context. The context suggests a gnomic reading.

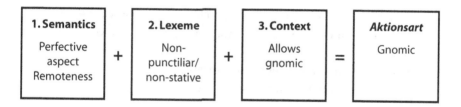

Perfect and Pluperfect Tense-Forms

For each passage, (1) write about the semantic meaning of the verb, (2) state the contribution of the lexeme, and (3) discuss the function of the verb in context. Once you have written your answers, summarize your findings in the boxes below each passage.

Example:

John 7:27 ἀλλὰ τοῦτον **οἴδαμεν** πόθεν ἐστίν· ὁ δὲ χριστὸς ὅταν ἔρχηται οὐδεὶς γινώσκει πόθεν ἐστίν.

But we know where this man is from. When the Christ comes, nobody will know where he is from.

1. Semantic meaning of the verb. The perfect indicative semantically encodes imperfective aspect and the spatial value of heightened proximity.

2. Contribution of the lexeme. The lexeme is stative.

3. Function in context. The context allows stativity.

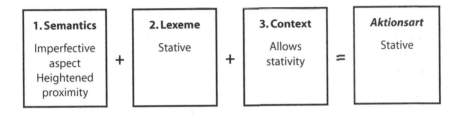

Romans 1:17 δικαιοσύνη γὰρ θεοῦ ἐν αὐτῷ ἀποκαλύπτεται ἐκ πίστεως εἰς πίστιν, καθὼς **γέγραπται**· ὁ δὲ δίκαιος ἐκ πίστεως ζήσεται.

*For in it God's righteousness is revealed from faith to faith, just as **it is written**: The righteous will live by faith.*

1. Semantic meaning of the verb. The perfect indicative semantically encodes imperfective aspect and the spatial value of heightened proximity.

2. Contribution of the lexeme. The lexeme is transitive.

3. Function in context. The context suggests stativity.

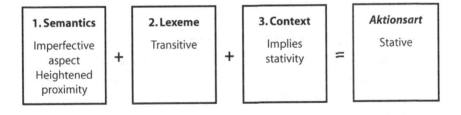

John 7:30 Ἐζήτουν οὖν αὐτὸν πιάσαι, καὶ οὐδεὶς ἐπέβαλεν ἐπ᾽ αὐτὸν τὴν χεῖρα, ὅτι **οὔπω ἐληλύθει** ἡ ὥρα αὐτοῦ.

*Then they tried to seize him. Yet no one laid a hand on him because his hour **had not yet come**.*

1. Semantic meaning of the verb. The pluperfect indicative semantically encodes imperfective aspect and the spatial value of heightened remoteness.

2. Contribution of the lexeme. The lexeme is intransitive.

3. Function in context. The context expresses past-past temporal reference.

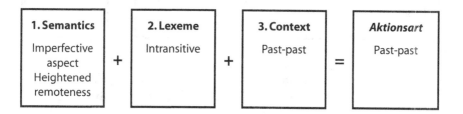

John 16:11 περὶ δὲ κρίσεως, ὅτι ὁ ἄρχων τοῦ κόσμου τούτου κέκριται.

*... and about judgment, because the ruler of this world **is being judged**.*

1. Semantic meaning of the verb. The perfect indicative semantically encodes imperfective aspect and the spatial value of heightened proximity.

2. Contribution of the lexeme. The lexeme is not punctiliar nor stative.

3. Function in context. The context allows progression.

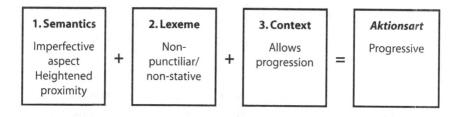

John 1:15 Ἰωάννης μαρτυρεῖ περὶ αὐτοῦ καὶ **κέκραγεν** λέγων· οὗτος ἦν ὃν εἶπον....

*John testified concerning him and **exclaimed**, "This was the one of whom I said ..."*

1. Semantic meaning of the verb. The perfect indicative semantically encodes imperfective aspect and the spatial value of heightened proximity.

2. Contribution of the lexeme. The lexeme introduces discourse.

3. Function in context. The context is past referring.

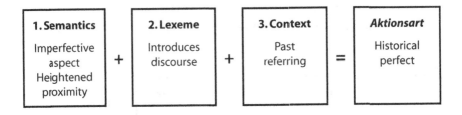

Romans 8:38 πέπεισμαι γὰρ ὅτι οὔτε θάνατος οὔτε ζωὴ οὔτε ἄγγελοι οὔτε ἀρχαὶ οὔτε ἐνεστῶτα οὔτε μέλλοντα οὔτε δυνάμεις

*For **I am persuaded** that neither death nor life, nor angels nor rulers, nor things present, nor things to come, nor powers...*

1. Semantic meaning of the verb. The perfect indicative semantically encodes imperfective aspect and the spatial value of heightened proximity.

2. Contribution of the lexeme. The lexeme is stative.

3. Function in context. The context allows stativity.

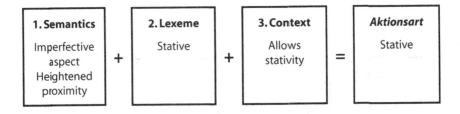

Matthew 7:25 καὶ κατέβη ἡ βροχὴ καὶ ἦλθον οἱ ποταμοὶ καὶ ἔπνευσαν οἱ ἄνεμοι καὶ προσέπεσαν τῇ οἰκίᾳ ἐκείνῃ, καὶ οὐκ ἔπεσεν, **τεθεμελίωτο** γὰρ ἐπὶ τὴν πέτραν.

*The rain fell, the rivers rose, and the winds blew and pounded that house. Yet it didn't collapse, because **it was founded** on the rock.*

1. Semantic meaning of the verb. The pluperfect indicative semantically encodes imperfective aspect and the spatial value of heightened remoteness.

2. Contribution of the lexeme. The lexeme is transitive.

3. Function in context. The context implies stativity.

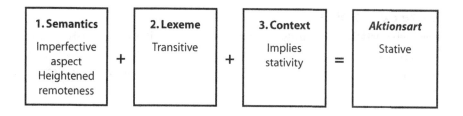

John 19:30 ὅτε οὖν ἔλαβεν τὸ ὄξος [ὁ] Ἰησοῦς εἶπεν· **τετέλεσται**, καὶ κλίνας τὴν κεφαλὴν παρέδωκεν τὸ πνεῦμα.

*When Jesus had received the sour wine, he said, "**It is finished!**" Then bowing his head, he gave up his spirit.*

1. Semantic meaning of the verb. The perfect indicative semantically encodes imperfective aspect and the spatial value of heightened proximity.
2. Contribution of the lexeme. The lexeme is transitive.
3. Function in context. The context implies stativity.

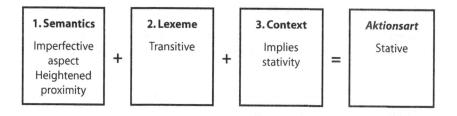

John 20:11 Μαρία δὲ **εἱστήκει** πρὸς τῷ μνημείῳ ἔξω κλαίουσα. ὡς οὖν ἔκλαιεν, παρέκυψεν εἰς τὸ μνημεῖον.

*But Mary **was standing** outside facing the tomb, crying. As she was crying, she stooped to look into the tomb.*

1. Semantic meaning of the verb. The pluperfect indicative semantically encodes imperfective aspect and the spatial value of heightened remoteness.
2. Contribution of the lexeme. The lexeme is stative.
3. Function in context. The context allows stativity.

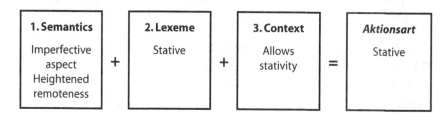

More Participles

For each participle encountered, work out whether it is periphrastic, adjectival, substantival, or a participle of attendant circumstance. Then identify the aspect of the participle, and describe what it is doing in the context.

Example:

John 16:5   νῦν δὲ ὑπάγω πρὸς τὸν **πέμψαντά** με, καὶ οὐδεὶς ἐξ ὑμῶν ἐρωτᾷ με· ποῦ ὑπάγεις;

*But now I am going away to the one **who sent** me, and not one of you asks me, "Where are you going?"*

1. Periphrastic, adjectival, substantival, or attendant circumstance? This participle is substantival.
2. What is the aspectual value? This aorist participle is perfective in aspect.
3. What is the participle doing in the context? This substantival participle conveys a nuance of past temporal reference.

John 5:2   Ἔστιν δὲ ἐν τοῖς Ἱεροσολύμοις ἐπὶ τῇ προβατικῇ κολυμβήθρα ἡ **ἐπιλεγομένη** Ἑβραϊστὶ Βηθζαθὰ πέντε στοὰς ἔχουσα.

*By the Sheep Gate in Jerusalem there is a pool, **called** Bethesda in Hebrew, which has five colonnades.*

1. Periphrastic, adjectival, substantival, or attendant circumstance? This participle is adjectival.
2. What is the aspectual value? This present participle is imperfective in aspect.
3. What is the participle doing in the context? This adjectival participle describes the noun it qualifies.

Luke 16:6   ὁ δὲ εἶπεν· ἑκατὸν βάτους ἐλαίου. ὁ δὲ εἶπεν αὐτῷ· δέξαι σου τὰ γράμματα καὶ **καθίσας** ταχέως γράψον πεντήκοντα.

*"A hundred measures of oil," he said. "Take your invoice," he told him, "**sit down** quickly, and write fifty."*

1. Periphrastic, adjectival, substantival, or attendant circumstance? This is a participle of attendant circumstance.
2. What is the aspectual value? This aorist participle is perfective in aspect.

3. What is the participle doing in the context? This participle conveys imperatival force.

John 13:23 ἦν **ἀνακείμενος** εἷς ἐκ τῶν μαθητῶν αὐτοῦ ἐν τῷ κόλπῳ τοῦ Ἰησοῦ, ὃν ἠγάπα ὁ Ἰησοῦς.

*One of his disciples, the one Jesus loved, was **reclining** close beside Jesus.*

1. Periphrastic, adjectival, substantival, or attendant circumstance? This participle forms an imperfect periphrasis.
2. What is the aspectual value? This present participle is imperfective in aspect.
3. What is the participle doing in the context? This participle combines with the imperfect auxiliary to provide the meaning of the imperfect periphrasis.

Romans 7:14 Οἴδαμεν γὰρ ὅτι ὁ νόμος πνευματικός ἐστιν, ἐγὼ δὲ σάρκινός εἰμι **πεπραμένος** ὑπὸ τὴν ἁμαρτίαν.

*For we know that the law is spiritual; but I am made out of flesh, **sold** into sin's power.*

1. Periphrastic, adjectival, substantival, or attendant circumstance? This participle is adjectival.
2. What is the aspectual value? This perfect participle is imperfective in aspect.
3. What is the participle doing in the context? This adjectival participle conveys a nuance of past temporal reference (with a verb of propulsion).

Acts 5:5 ἀκούων δὲ ὁ Ἀνανίας τοὺς λόγους τούτους **πεσὼν** ἐξέψυξεν, καὶ ἐγένετο φόβος μέγας ἐπὶ πάντας τοὺς ἀκούοντας.

*When he heard these words, Ananias **dropped** dead, and a great fear came on all who heard.*

1. Periphrastic, adjectival, substantival, or attendant circumstance? This is a participle of attendant circumstance.
2. What is the aspectual value? This aorist participle is perfective in aspect.
3. What is the participle doing in the context? This participle conveys the force of an aorist indicative.

John 3:24 οὔπω γὰρ ἦν **βεβλημένος** εἰς τὴν φυλακὴν ὁ Ἰωάννης.

*. . . for John had not yet **been thrown** into prison.*

1. Periphrastic, adjectival, substantival, or attendant circumstance? This participle forms a pluperfect periphrasis.

2. What is the aspectual value? This perfect participle is imperfective in aspect.

3. What is the participle doing in the context? This perfect participle combines with the imperfect auxiliary to form a pluperfect periphrasis.

Mark 14:69 καὶ ἡ παιδίσκη ἰδοῦσα αὐτὸν ἤρξατο πάλιν λέγειν τοῖς **παρεστῶσιν** ὅτι οὗτος ἐξ αὐτῶν ἐστιν.

*When the servant saw him again she began to tell those **standing** nearby, "This man is one of them!"*

1. Periphrastic, adjectival, substantival, or attendant circumstance? This is a substantive participle.

2. What is the aspectual value? This perfect participle is imperfective in aspect.

3. What is the participle doing in the context? This participle conveys a nuance of contemporaneous temporal reference.Scripture Index

Scripture Index

Subject Index